an ASCD ActionTOOL

EDUCATING THE
Whole Child

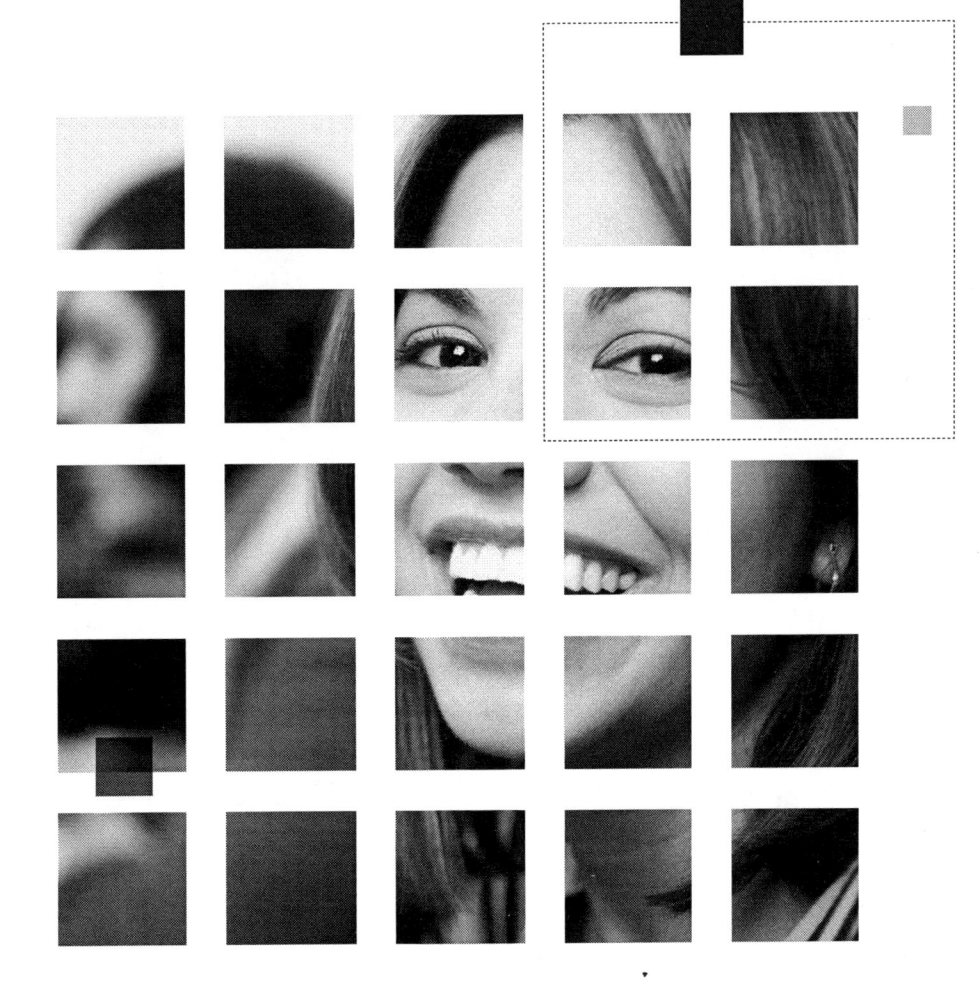

ASCD

ASSOCIATION FOR SUPERVISION
AND CURRICULUM DEVELOPMENT

Alexandria, Virginia USA

ASCD

Association for Supervision and Curriculum Development
1703 North Beauregard Street
Alexandria, VA 22311-1714 USA
Phone: 1-800-933-2723 or 1-703-578-9600
Fax: 1-703-575-5400
Web site: www.ascd.org

Author
John L. Brown

ASCD Staff
ASCD's Executive Director is Gene R. Carter.

Content Production
Ann Cunningham-Morris, Director, Professional Development
Theresa Lewallen, Director, Healthy School Communities
Tamera Anderson, Project Specialist
Leslie Welch, Project Coordinator
Anedra Edwards, Intern

Manual Production
Gary Bloom, Director, Design and Production Services
Greer Beeken, Senior Graphic Designer
Mike Kalyan, Production Manager
EEI Communications, Desktop Publishing

ASCD is a membership organization that develops programs, products, and services essential to the way educators learn, teach, and lead. Founded in 1943, ASCD is a worldwide education association with headquarters in Alexandria, Virginia, USA.

ASCD publications present a variety of viewpoints. The views expressed or implied in the manual should not be interpreted as official positions of the Association.

Copyright 2008 by the Association for Supervision and Curriculum Development, 1703 North Beauregard Street, Alexandria, Virginia 22311-1714. All rights reserved. Materials of this guide are intended for use in meetings, professional development opportunities, classrooms, and school community gatherings. For this purpose, materials in these sections of the guide may be reproduced. Any other use of these materials is prohibited, unless written permission is granted by ASCD.

Printed in the United States of America.
ASCD Stock No: 709036
ISBN: 978-1-4166-0788-5
ASCD member price: $69   Nonmember price: $89

15 14 13 12 11 10 09 08   10 9 8 7 6 5 4 3 2 1

Educating the Whole Child
An ASCD Action Tool

John L. Brown

Educating the Whole Child
An ASCD Action Tool

About ASCD vi

About the Author viii

Acknowledgments ix

Downloads x

Introduction 1

Organization of This Action Tool 3

OVERVIEW
Engaging Stakeholders: Beginning Your Whole Child Strategic
Planning Process 7

TENET ONE
Entering School Healthy and Promoting Healthy Schools
and Healthy Lifestyles 65

TENET TWO
Creating Intellectually Challenging Learning Environments
That Are Physically and Emotionally Safe 95

TENET THREE
Ensuring Active Student Engagement and Connectedness 125

TENET FOUR
Personalizing the Learning Process and Ensuring All Learners
Work with Qualified, Caring Adults 151

TENET FIVE
Preparing Each Student for College, Postgraduation Study,
and Work in a Global Environment 179

Putting It All Together 213

References and Other Resources 257

About ASCD

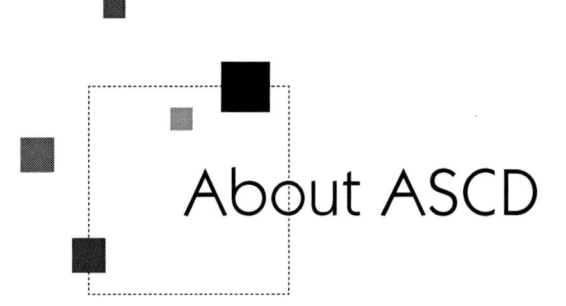

Founded in 1943, the Association for Supervision and Curriculum Development (ASCD) is a nonpartisan, nonprofit education association, with international headquarters in Alexandria, Virginia. ASCD's Mission Statement: ASCD is a membership organization that develops programs, products, and services essential to the way educators learn, teach, and lead.

Membership in ASCD includes a subscription to the award-winning journal *Educational Leadership,* the *Education Update* newsletter, and other products and services. ASCD sponsors affiliate organizations around the world; participates in collaborations and networks; holds conferences, institutes, and training programs; produces publications in a variety of media; sponsors recognition and awards programs; and provides research information on education issues.

ASCD provides many services to educators—prekindergarten through grade 12—as well as to others in the education community, including parents, school board members, administrators, and university professors and students. For further information, contact ASCD via telephone: 1-800-933-2723 or 1-703-578-9600; fax: 1-703-575-5400; or e-mail: member@ascd.org. Or write to ASCD, Information Services, 1703 N. Beauregard Street, Alexandria, VA 22311-1714 USA. You can find ASCD on the World Wide Web at www.ascd.org. ASCD's Executive Director is Gene R. Carter.

2008–09 Board of Directors

Valerie Truesdale (President), Linda Mariotti (President-Elect), Nancy DeFord (Immediate Past President), Robert Bruckner, Jaime Castellano, Becky Cooke, Henry Tyrone Harris, Paul Healey, Denise Hernandez, Katherine H. Howard, Marsha Jones, Donald Kachur, Roland Kay, Betsy Lim, James Lombardo, Mary Ravita, Yolanda M. Rey, Realista Rodriguez, Mark Sutter, Wayne C. Sweeney, Carlos A. Viera

Belief Statements

Fundamental to ASCD is our concern for people, both individually and collectively.

- We believe that the individual has intrinsic worth.
- We believe that all people have the ability and the need to learn.
- We believe that all children have a right to safety, love, and learning.
- We believe that a high-quality, public system of education open to all is imperative for society to flourish.
- We believe that diversity strengthens society and should be honored and protected.
- We believe that broad, informed participation committed to a common good is critical to democracy.
- We believe that humanity prospers when people work together.

ASCD also recognizes the potential and power of a healthy organization.

- We believe that healthy organizations purposefully provide for self-renewal.
- We believe that the culture of an organization is a major factor shaping individual attitudes and behaviors.
- We believe that shared values and common goals shape and change the culture of healthy organizations.

About the Author

John L. Brown is currently an education consultant with the Association for Supervision and Curriculum Development. In that capacity, he is a member of two national training cadres: Understanding by Design and What Works in Schools. He has also published a wide range of materials for ASCD, including the best-selling book *Making the Most of Understanding by Design,* as well as *The Hero's Journey: A Personal Guide to Transforming Schools and Observing Dimensions of Learning in Classrooms and Schools.* He is the author of numerous other ASCD publications, action tools, and online courses on the following topics: balanced assessment; standards-based grading and assessment; curriculum development, renewal, and alignment; Dimensions of Learning; Understanding by Design; What Works in Schools; Schooling by Design; and Teaching Thinking Skills.

Brown has also served as an education consultant to schools and districts throughout the United States, Canada, Bermuda, and Barbados on a wide variety of topics, including curriculum design and mapping, unpacking standards, performance-based assessment and instruction, research-based teaching-learning strategies, and learning styles. He is an expert in working with schools and districts to design and develop curriculum in all content areas as well as strategic plans for improving student achievement. In addition to his work as an education consultant for ASCD, Brown has served as a director of professional development and program development, and as a specialist in Gifted and Talented Education in Prince George's County Public Schools, Maryland. He has taught English at the high school and college levels and curriculum development at Trinity College (Washington, D.C.), Johns Hopkins University, and Western Maryland College.

Brown received his PhD in education from George Mason University and master's and bachelor's degrees in English from the University of Wisconsin, Madison. His awards include Outstanding Educator, 1993, and Outstanding Maryland High School English Teacher, 1986.

Acknowledgments

This action tool is an outgrowth of the powerful contributions of the individuals who were instrumental in bringing about the collective vision, principles, and conceptual tenets associated with the ASCD's Whole Child Initiative. In particular, we wish to express our sincere gratitude to the members of the Commission on the Whole Child, authors of *The Learning Compact Redefined: A Call to Action,* which laid the groundwork for this action tool. We are indebted to all of the members of that Commission: Frederick J. Bramante Jr., Peter Cobb, James Comer, Elliott Eisner, Edward B. Fiske, John Goodlad, Stedman Graham, Jonathan Jansen, Sharon Kagan, Lawrence Kohn, Lloyd J. Kolbe, Stephanie Pace Marshall (Cochair), Myles Miller, Monte C. Moses, Nel Noddings, Pedro Noguera, Hugh Price (Cochair), Kate Quarfordt, Suellen Reed, and Doris Williams.

The author also wishes to express his sincere appreciation to the following ASCD staff members for their generous support during the development of this publication: Maxine Bane, Jennifer Barrett, Debbie Brown, Ann Cunningham-Morris, Diane Jackson, Theresa Lewallen, Ben Licciardi, Molly McCloskey, Ron Miletta, Andrea Palmiter, Judy Seltz, David Snyder, Mikki Terry, Leslie Welch, and Kathy Welling.

Downloads

The supporting *Educational Leadership* articles and electronic versions of the tools are available for download at **www.ascd.org/downloads**.

Enter this unique key to unlock the files:
GAE6C-019FA-03612-91640-00100G

If you have difficulty accessing the files, email webhelp@ascd.org or call 1-800-933-ASCD for assistance.

© 2008. All Rights Reserved.

Introduction

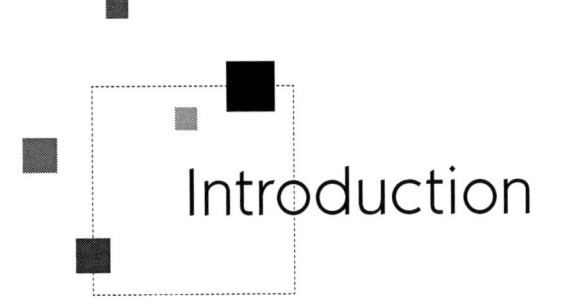

The Association for Supervision and Curriculum Development (ASCD) convened the Commission on the Whole Child in January and July 2006. Composed of leading thinkers, researchers, and practitioners from a wide variety of sectors, the Commission was charged with recasting the definition of a successful learner from one whose achievement is measured solely by academic tests to one who is knowledgeable, emotionally and physically healthy, civically inspired, engaged in the arts, prepared for work and economic self-sufficiency, and ready for the world beyond formal schooling.

According to ASCD Executive Director Gene Carter, "ASCD convened the Commission on the Whole Child because we believe that the success of each learner can only be achieved through a whole child approach to learning and teaching. If decisions about education policy and practice started by asking what works for the child, how would resources—time, space, and human—be arrayed to ensure each child's success? If the student were truly at the center of the system, what could we achieve?"

In 2007, at the completion of the initial work of the Commission, ASCD published *The Learning Compact Redefined: A Call to Action,* identifying the major structural components of the Whole Child Initiative. This report advocates a comprehensive approach to learning and teaching. The Whole Child Compact emphasizes that successful young people must not only be knowledgeable when they graduate from school, but also emotionally and physically healthy, civically engaged, responsible, and caring. It asserts that every child deserves a 21st century education that fully prepares him or her for college, work, and citizenship.

The Whole Child Compact identified the major components or "tenets" that form the infrastructure of the ASCD's Whole Child Initiative:

- Each student enters school healthy and learns about and practices a healthy lifestyle.
- Each student learns in an intellectually challenging environment that is physically and emotionally safe for students and adults.

- Each student is actively engaged in learning and is connected to the school and broader community.
- Each student has access to personalized learning and is supported by qualified, caring adults.
- Each graduate is prepared for success in college or further study and for employment in a global environment.

This publication, *Educating the Whole Child: An ASCD Action Tool,* represents the next step in helping educators, families, and community stakeholders to realize the vision of an educational system dedicated to the welfare and development of the whole child. Presenting a comprehensive set of tools and resources related to each of the five Whole Child tenets, this publication includes suggestions for community conversations (i.e., interactive dialogues and strategic planning sessions involving key stakeholders); professional development; school improvement planning; and sustaining stakeholder support and engagement. These resources are intended to be practical and useful tools to enable every school and district to become positive communities of learning that ensure every student is

- intellectually active
- physically, verbally, socially, and academically competent
- empathetic, kind, caring, and fair
- creative and curious
- disciplined, self-directed, and goal oriented
- free
- a critical thinker
- confident
- cared for and valued

Ideally, the materials, resources, and suggestions presented in this publication will help stakeholders move their learning organizations from establishing an initial vision for the whole child toward concretely bringing that vision to reality. Perhaps most significant, we hope that this resource can become a catalyst for ensuring the longevity and value added of the structural, organizational, policy, and human interaction patterns associated with true and successful Whole Child transformation.

Organization of This Action Tool

This action tool presents a comprehensive process for use by school-based, district-level, and community stakeholders interested in putting into operation the principles and recommendations of ASCD's Whole Child initiative. It includes a range of resources for promoting community conversations, professional development, and strategic planning related to core Whole Child tenets. Through these processes, users will be able to respond to the essential questions at the heart of ASCD's *Learning Compact Redefined*:

1. How can we ensure that each student enters school healthy and learns about and practices a healthy lifestyle?
2. How can we help each student learn in an intellectually challenging environment that is physically and emotionally safe for students and adults?
3. How can we be certain that each student is actively engaged in learning and is— connected to the school and broader community?
4. How can we ensure that each student has access to personalized learning and to qualified, caring adults?
5. How can we prepare each graduate for success in college or further study and for employment in a global environment?

This action tool begins with suggestions and resources for individual users and groups to reflect upon the ways in which their current school improvement team is addressing Whole Child tenets and intervention strategies as part of its strategic planning process. Based upon this initial evaluation, users may then form an independent Whole Child strategic planning team using the tools and suggestions presented in this section, or use the tools in this resource to complement their existing school improvement planning process. This first section, "Engaging Stakeholders: Beginning Your Whole Child Strategic Planning Process," profiles each of the major focus areas, strategic planning methodologies, and categories of resources that are presented in each of the subsequent sections dealing with the five individual Whole Child tenets:

- Recommendations for key components of the Whole Child strategic planning process
- Suggestions for determining the vision, mission, and guiding principles of your Whole Child strategic planning team (either as an independent structure or as a complement to your existing school improvement planning team)
- Ideas for structuring and ensuring the success of your Whole Child strategic planning team
- Promoting communication within and outside your Whole Child strategic planning team
- Beginning your Whole Child needs analysis process
- Engaging stakeholders through Community Conversations
- Creating your vision for education to prepare each child for the 21st century
- Whole Child professional development principles (i.e., taking stakeholders from initial orientation training sessions toward job-embedded collaborative inquiry)
- Whole Child study group methodology
- Inquiry teams and Whole Child problem solving and decision making
- Whole Child action research
- Key elements of the Whole Child strategic planning process
- Promoting and sustaining community outreach and stakeholder involvement in your Whole Child transformation process

This action tool is divided into sections designed to "unpack" and to help users implement key elements of each of the Whole Child tenets. Each section contains materials and resources to support the planning and implementation of Whole Child practices and policies.

Electronic Tools and Resources

Educational Leadership articles and interactive versions of the tools are available for download. To access these documents, navigate your Internet browser to www.ascd.org/downloads. If you are having difficulties viewing the files, contact webhelp@ascd.org for assistance or call 1-800-933-ASCD. All files are saved in Adobe Portable Document Format (PDF). The PDF file is compatible with both personal computers (PCs) and Macintosh computers. **Note: You must have the Adobe Acrobat Professional software on your machine to save your work.** The main menu will let you navigate through the various sections, and you can print individual tools or sections in their entirety.

The purchase of this action tool also provides one-time access to the ASCD Whole Child Survey, an online tool that will support the planning and implementation of the Whole Child framework. Instructions on accessing the online tool are sent to purchasers by email.

Minimum System Requirements

Program: The most current version of the Adobe Reader software is available for free download at www.adobe.com.

PC: Intel Pentium Processor; Microsoft Windows XP Professional or Home Edition (Service Pack 1 or 2), Windows 2000 (Service Pack 2), Windows XP Tablet PC Edition, Windows Server 2003, or Windows NT (Service Pack 6 or 6a); 128 MB of RAM (256 MB recommended); up to 90 MB of available hard-disk space; Internet Explorer 5.5 (or higher), Netscape 7.1 (or higher), Firefox 1.0, or Mozilla 1.7.

Macintosh: PowerPC G3, G4, or G5 processor, Mac OS X v.10.2.8–10.3; 128 MB of RAM (256 MB recommended); up to 110 MB of available hard-disk space; Safari 1.2.2 browser supported for MAC OS X 10.3 or higher.

Getting Started

Select download files. Designate a location on your computer to save the files. Choose to launch the PDF presentation with your existing version of Adobe Acrobat Reader or install the newest version of Adobe Acrobat Reader from www.adobe.com. From the Main Menu, select a section by clicking on its title. To view a specific tool, open the Bookmarks tab in the left navigation pane and then click on the title of the tool.

Entering and Saving Text

To enter text on the form, position your cursor inside a form field and click. The pointer will change to an I-beam to allow you to enter text. If the pointer changes to a pointing finger, you can select a check box or radio button. Press Enter or Return to create a paragraph return in the field. Press Tab or use your mouse to move between fields. To cancel an entry, press the Escape button to restore the previous text or to deselect a field. **Remember, you must have Adobe Acrobat Professional to save your work.**

Printing Tools

To print a single tool, select the tool by clicking on its title via the Bookmarks section and click on the printer icon or select File then Print. In the Print Range section, select Current Page to print the page on the screen. To print several tools, enter the page range in the "Pages from" field. If you wish to print all of the tools in the section, select All in the Printer Range section, then click OK.

OVERVIEW TOOLS

Engaging Stakeholders: Beginning Your Whole Child Strategic Planning Process

INTRODUCTION

Strategic Planning and Your Whole Child Initiative 9

TITLE OF TOOL

1. Determining the Mission and Guiding Principles of Your Team. 13

2. Determining Key Components of Your Whole Child Strategic Planning Team . . 17

3. Promoting Communication Within and Outside Your Whole Child Strategic Planning Team. 19

4. Beginning Your Whole Child Needs Analysis Process. 23

5. Engaging Stakeholders Through Community Conversations—Where Are We? Where Do We Need to Go?. 27

6. Creating and Sharing Your Vision for Education to Prepare Each Child for the 21st Century 31

TITLE OF TOOL

7. Whole Child Professional Development Principles. 37

8. Whole Child Study Group. 41

9. Inquiry Teams and Whole Child Problem-Solving and
   Decision-Making Processes 45

10. The Whole Child Action Research Process. 49

11. Key Elements of the Whole Child Strategic Planning Process. 53

12. Sustaining Community Support and Collaboration 59

Strategic Planning and Your Whole Child Initiative

Whether you decide to work with Whole Child tenets, principles, and processes by integrating them into your existing school improvement team or you elect to form a parallel Whole Child planning team responsible for overseeing the process, your approach should include 10 essential steps that will help you to realize your Whole Child vision:

☐ **STEP 1 | Determine the Goals of Your Whole Child Initiative**

Identify the vision for educating the whole child.

☐ **STEP 2 | Conduct Community Conversations**

Guide key stakeholders in Community Conversation(s) to explore the following:

- The vision for educating the whole child
- The long-range and short-term priorities
- The stakeholder collaboration needed to achieve the shared vision

☐ **STEP 3 | Build Momentum for Your Whole Child Initiative**

Key stakeholders conduct follow-up orientation, group discussion, and exploration activities involving students, families, community members, business and government representatives, and other relevant groups and individuals.

☐ **STEP 4 | Form Your Whole Child Strategic Planning Team**

Develop your Whole Child planning team involving representatives from all relevant stakeholder groups. Include identification of members, delineation of roles, responsibilities, and design of time line.

☐ **STEP 5 | Collect and Analyze Whole Child Baseline Data**

Planning team collects data to assess the current status of meeting the Whole Child vision.

☐ **STEP 6 | Build Consensus Among Stakeholders Regarding Immediate and Long-Range Goals**

Planning team builds consensus among stakeholders and then finalizes short-term and long-range priorities, goals, and annual performance targets.

☐ STEP 7 | Develop Your Multiyear Whole Child Strategic Plan

Planning team develops a multiyear plan incorporating your Whole Child vision, goals, annual performance targets, suggested data sources, action plan, professional development plan, outreach and engagement activities, and suggestions for cross-tenet alignment.

☐ STEP 8 | Develop and Implement Job-Embedded Professional Development

Under the guidance and oversight of your Whole Child planning team, professional development may include the following:

- Initial orientation workshops,
- Study group activities,
- Inquiry team discussions and investigations,
- Action research projects, and
- Related learning sessions for relevant stakeholder groups (e.g., students, families, community members, business/corporate community, health and human service organizations, and postsecondary educational institutions).

☐ STEP 9 | Sustain Momentum

The team works with stakeholders to determine the impact of the Whole Child implementation process by using a collaborative action research approach for each component of the strategic plan:

- Distribute leadership by allowing stakeholders to assume responsibility for implementation.
- Engage stakeholders in action research and inquiry focused on the plan.
- During implementation, revisit goals and actions.
- Modify the plan appropriately.
- Continue to share insights, recommendations, and suggestions for expanding use of effective strategies and practices.
- Communicate changes to stakeholders.

☐ STEP 10 | Determine Impact and Celebrate Success of Your Whole Child Initiative

Throughout the multiyear Whole Child implementation process, the strategic planning team collaborates with relevant individuals and groups to collect and analyze student achievement and organizational performance data to determine the following:

- What have we accomplished? To what extent have we achieved our long-range goals and identified performance targets?
- How has our Whole Child Initiative affected each of our students?
- How has our learning organization changed as a result of our work?

Make a commitment to ensure that successes are acknowledged publicly and that all stakeholders have the opportunity to celebrate success.

Planning Tips to Keep in Mind

1. Consider planning with multiple school sites that form a community feeder pattern; you will need a cross-institutional planning team to provide oversight for the process.
2. Ensure ongoing involvement among all key stakeholder groups in your community.
3. Continually examine and revisit how the Whole Child tenets are interconnected and interrelated within your learning community. Avoid unnaturally separating them into segregated silos.
4. Acknowledge and celebrate the Whole Child tenets and practices that may already be operational in your organization.

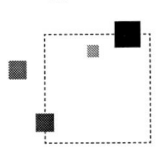

Action Tool One: Determining the Mission and Guiding Principles of Your Team

PURPOSE OF THIS TOOL

Just as a school mission establishes what that learning organization is in business to accomplish, your Whole Child strategic planning team can begin its work by articulating its own mission and key operating principles. This tool will help your team to articulate its purpose and guiding principles. Using this tool, you will be able to summarize the specific intended effects of your work and your aims for the school as a Whole Child learning organization.

HOW TO USE THIS TOOL

Your Whole Child strategic planning process can begin with a group of interested stakeholders reviewing the highlights of the Whole Child Compact. This tool will help group members come to consensus about their purpose and guiding principles for addressing the five Whole Child tenets. They can use this tool to summarize their long-term aims, against which stakeholders will design and adjust their work with this initiative. In effect, the team's mission should summarize its governing purpose within the school or district.

TIPS AND VARIATIONS

- ✓ Once your Whole Child team has developed the initial draft of its mission and related operating principles, it can share them with other relevant stakeholders in the school or district.
- ✓ Use the finalized team mission as a tool for stakeholder groups to judge the level of organizational change occurring as a result of your Whole Child strategic planning process.

Determining the Mission and Guiding Principles of Your Team

DIRECTIONS:

Appoint a group facilitator responsible for leading your team's discussion about the Whole Child. Under each section, record the big ideas the team agrees should be part of its mission.

According to the Whole Child Compact, a whole child is

- intellectually active
- physically, verbally, socially, and academically competent
- empathetic, kind, caring, and fair
- creative and curious
- disciplined, self-directed, and goal oriented
- free
- a critical thinker
- confident
- cared for and valued

Our team agrees that the following big ideas from this list should become a part of our team mission statement:

The Five Tenets of the Whole Child Compact:
- Each student enters school healthy and learns about and practices a healthy lifestyle.
- Each student learns in an intellectually challenging environment that is physically and emotionally safe for students and adults.
- Each student is actively engaged in learning and is connected to the school and broader community.
- Each student has access to personalized learning and to qualified, caring adults.
- Each graduate is prepared for success in college or further study and for employment in a global environment.

What are the big ideas in the Whole Child Compact that our team members wish to emphasize as part of our team mission statement and guiding principles?

Action Tool One: Determining the Mission and Guiding Principles of Your Team

To develop the whole child requires that communities provide
- Family support and involvement
- Government, civic, and business support and resources
- Volunteers and advocates
- Support for their districts' coordinated school health councils or other collaborative structures

We agree that the following big ideas from this list be included in our team mission statement and guiding principles:

To develop the whole child requires that schools provide
- Challenging and engaging curriculum
- Adequate professional development with collaborative planning time embedded within the school day
- A safe, healthy, orderly, and trusting environment
- High-quality teachers and other staff (e.g., nurses, counselors, coaches, custodians) and administrators
- A climate that supports strong relationships between adults and students
- Support for coordinated school health councils or other collaborative structures that are active in the school

We agree that the following big ideas from this list be included in our team mission statement and guiding principles:

To develop the whole child requires that teachers provide
- Evidence-based assessment and instructional practices
- Rich content and an engaging learning climate
- Student and family connectedness
- Effective classroom management
- Modeling of healthy behaviors

We agree that the following big ideas from this list be included in our team mission statement and guiding principles:

Action Tool One: Determining the Mission and Guiding Principles of Your Team

DIRECTIONS:

Use the big idea discussion results to finalize your Whole Child strategic planning team's mission and to articulate the guiding principles you will adopt to guide and inform your long-term Whole Child work.

Finalizing the Elements of Your Whole Child Team's Mission Statement
If we are successful, each of our graduates will
If we are successful, our community will
If we are successful, each of our schools will
If we are successful, each of our teachers will

Our Whole Child Team Mission Statement
As a result of our long-term commitment to the whole child:

Guiding Principles for Our Whole Child Team
To achieve this mission, we dedicate ourselves to the following guiding principles:

© 2008. All Rights Reserved.

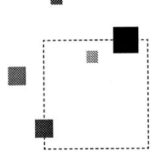

Action Tool Two: Determining Key Components of Your Whole Child Strategic Planning Team

PURPOSE OF THIS TOOL

As your Whole Child strategic planning team begins its work, this tool will provide a planning guide to support its key structural elements. Use the guide to help determine team membership, the range of roles and responsibilities team members will assume, long- and short-range goals for team operations, and logistical and resource commitments and requirements. Remember to use your team mission and guiding principles to inform the direction of your work and the processes you will use to complete it.

HOW TO USE THIS TOOL

Begin by selecting strategic planning team members based on their interests, experiences, expertise, and time commitments. A key operating principle is to ensure that all relevant stakeholder groups have representation within this group. This tool can also help you to explore the issue of the team's relationship to your overall organizational structure: Is it to function as a complement to your school improvement planning team, or will it have some level of autonomy? Remember that as the work of the team begins, roles and responsibilities will evolve, just as ongoing modifications will need to be made to outcomes, methods, and team membership.

TIPS AND VARIATIONS

- ✓ Consider such important issues as leadership and available resources as you begin your work. For example, to what extent does the school or district sanction your mission, guiding principles, and goals? How will your work be supported by teachers, administrators, central office personnel, families, and community members?
- ✓ Perhaps most important, as you begin to develop and implement your team and its operations, consider the breadth or scope of your initial and long-range work. For example, will you tackle issues related to each of the five tenets identified in the Whole Child Compact, or will you target key priorities related to the most pressing student and organizational needs?

Determining Key Components of Your Whole Child Strategic Planning Team

Initial Action Plan for a Whole Child Strategic Planning Team: _____ (Participating Schools)
1. Names and Positions of Team Members:
2. Team Mission:
3. Guiding Principles for Team Operations:
4. Suggested Whole Child Priority Areas:
5. Proposed Long-Range Goals:
6. Preliminary Annual Performance Targets:
7. Suggested Data Sources Related to Goals and Annual Performance Targets:
8. Initial Recommendations for Action Planning Priorities and Time Line:
9. Suggestions for Aligning Our Whole Child Team Work with School Improvement Planning in Participating School(s):
10. Projected Resources Needed (e.g., scheduling, time, support for Community Conversations, facilities, technology):

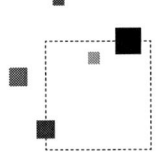

Action Tool Three: Promoting Communication Within and Outside Your Whole Child Strategic Planning Team

PURPOSE OF THIS TOOL

A recurrent priority for determining the success of your Whole Child strategic planning team is that it operate collaboratively with all major stakeholders within your learning organization and the community it serves. Your team must also make certain that its work complements—rather than works at cross-purposes with—the activities associated with your school improvement or districtwide strategic planning processes. This tool is designed to provide suggestions for promoting communication both within and outside your team. At the heart of this resource is the goal of keeping lines of communication open and eliminating unnecessary competitiveness or misalignment of initiatives and efforts.

HOW TO USE THIS TOOL

Use the rating scale and indicators provided in this tool to identify communication processes that your team members consider important for your work. Discuss which of the processes should be used for all aspects of team operations. Consider also which of the strategies and processes presented here may be especially useful at key junctures or benchmark points in your team's work together (e.g., during Community Conversations, presentations to stakeholder groups). Incorporate the final results of this process into your team's action plan.

TIPS AND VARIATIONS

- ✓ You may wish to classify various strategies for use with different team functions and operations. For example, you might discuss and adopt different conflict resolution strategies for internal events such as a team meeting versus external events such as a Community Conversation.
- ✓ Along with sustaining open communication within and outside team operations, consider issues extending from varying roles and responsibilities. Will the same leader serve as the head of your team throughout a particular academic year, or will leadership roles and responsibilities vary? Consider the communication implications of shifting roles and responsibilities.
- ✓ Finally, consider how communication will occur as your Whole Child strategic planning team interfaces with other committees and teams within your learning organization. How will you achieve consensus with other groups about communication processes, including decision-making and problem-solving approaches you will adopt?

Promoting Communication Within and Outside Your Whole Child Strategic Planning Team

DIRECTIONS:

1. Have each of your team members rate the level of importance they give to each of the recommended communication processes and strategies identified below: 4 = Highly significant for all aspects of team operations; 3 = Significant for most aspects of team operations; 2 = Significant for some aspects of team operations, but not for others; 1 = Potentially useful but not necessary for most aspects of team operations; 0 = Not important for any aspects of team operations.
2. Next, have team members share their ratings and create a data display using the matrix provided.
3. At the conclusion of your initial discussion, use a voting system (e.g., dot voting, hands raised) to build consensus about communication processes you will incorporate into your Whole Child action plan.
4. Be prepared to resolve any areas in which you have not achieved consensus.
5. Use the consensus template to summarize and distribute the decisions made.

Communication Process and Related Strategies	Rating (4–0)
1. Active listening: balanced and accurate summarizing and paraphrasing of team members' ideas and assertions	4 3 2 1 0
2. Nonverbal communication: eye contact, gestures, nodding	4 3 2 1 0
3. Written notes and summaries (internal): ensuring that all team members receive copies of meeting notes, agendas, and other materials	4 3 2 1 0
4. External written and electronic communication: ensuring that external stakeholders receive timely updates, reports, and so forth	4 3 2 1 0
5. Technology-based communication: ensuring that communication is maximized through use of appropriate technology-based sources (e.g., Internet, intranet, Web sites)	4 3 2 1 0
6. Group dynamics process observation: varying the role of process observer to ensure that fair and equitable opportunities exist for all members to be understood accurately and objectively	4 3 2 1 0
7. Conflict resolution processes: ensuring that the team agrees to use objective and mediated strategies and processes when conflicts develop or unresolved issues impede progress	4 3 2 1 0
8. Collaborative decision making: using an objective and data-driven process to arrive at consensus-driven conclusions and decisions related to team priorities and operations	4 3 2 1 0

Communication Process and Related Strategies (continued)	Rating (4–0)
9. Collaborative problem solving: identifying barriers and impediments and using consensus-driven and objective approaches to resolving significant group or organizational problems	4 3 2 1 0
10. Strategic planning: developing and implementing a data-driven strategic plan that guides and informs team operations and reinforces open and professional lines of communication	4 3 2 1 0
11. Cross-team interfacing: ensuring that our team does not operate in isolation, but actively interacts and interfaces with other teams working on related issues and priorities	4 3 2 1 0
12. Cross-team partnerships: building collaborative relationships and structures with other teams and cadres to ensure that our team reinforces a holistic, unified approach to Whole Child school reform	4 3 2 1 0
13. Promoting organizational alignment: making alignment between our Whole Child work, school improvement planning, and other organization reform initiatives a major priority for our team	4 3 2 1 0
14. Ensuring open and professional lines of communication between and among team leaders, team members, and stakeholder individuals and groups outside the team	4 3 2 1 0

CONSENSUS TEMPLATE

1. Based upon this process, we recommend that the following strategies become a regular part of our team meetings:

2. We recommend that the following strategies be emphasized when communicating outside our team:

3. We suggest that the following strategies be adopted for aligning our work with other teams and cadres within our learning organization:

4. We need to revisit the following issues related to internal and external communication involving our Whole Child strategic planning team:

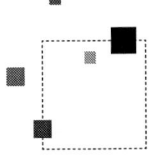

Action Tool Four: Beginning Your Whole Child Needs Analysis Process

PURPOSE OF THIS TOOL

Data acquisition and analysis should become a major resource and ongoing process as your team begins its work. In the sections of this action tool devoted to each of the five Whole Child tenets, you will find ideas and strategies for specific data analysis. This tool, however, is designed to encourage initial team brainstorming about potential data sources that may be used to finalize Whole Child priorities.

HOW TO USE THIS TOOL

At one of your earliest Whole Child team meetings, use this matrix to brainstorm and discuss responses to the following key needs analysis questions: (1) To what degree do we know the status of the major Whole Child components in our school or district? (2) What preliminary data sources are available to us to determine areas of strength and areas in which there may be gaps or omissions? (3) How can we access and analyze data from identified sources to begin to formulate our team priorities, including our long-range goals and annual performance targets?

TIPS AND VARIATIONS

- ✓ At the conclusion of your team's discussion of their responses to this action-planning matrix, use your results to plan next steps: What data sources already exist? To what extent do they provide us with sufficient data to determine action-planning priorities, including long-range goals and annual performance indicators?
- ✓ Explore ideas for finding or creating additional data sources where none currently exist.

Beginning Your Whole Child Needs Analysis Process

Whole Child Tenet	Data We Have	Data We Need
Tenet One: Each student enters school healthy.		
Tenet One: Our staff members model healthy practices for our students.		
Tenet One: Our school reflects the characteristics of a healthy building.		
Tenet One: Our students make healthy choices and demonstrate healthy lifestyles.		
Tenet Two: Each of our students is intellectually challenged while learning.		
Tenet Two: Our school is physically safe for all members of our learning community.		
Tenet Two: Our school is emotionally safe for all members of our learning community.		

Whole Child Tenet	Data We Have	Data We Need
Tenet Three: Each of our students is actively engaged in the learning process.		
Tenet Three: Each of our students is connected to the school as a learning community.		
Tenet Four: The learning process is personalized for each of our students.		
Tenet Four: Each of our students works with qualified, caring adults.		
Tenet Five: Each of our graduates is prepared for postsecondary education (i.e., college, university, other postsecondary educational institution).		
Tenet Five: Each of our graduates is prepared for success in the 21st century workplace.		

Final Recommendations: Based on our reactions to each of the elements of the five Whole Child tenets, what can we recommend for (1) our Whole Child priority areas, (2) areas in which we need additional data and data sources, and (3) next steps (including roles and responsibilities for our team)?

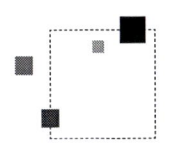

Action Tool Five: Engaging Stakeholders Through Community Conversations—Where Are We? Where Do We Need to Go?

PURPOSE OF THIS TOOL

Many schools and districts have already conducted Community Conversations as a starting point for their work with the Whole Child strategic planning process. Others may be just beginning. The resources in Action Tool Five present a summary of the process for developing and conducting Community Conversations. For a more detailed resource for this component of Whole Child work, we refer you to the ASCD online publication the *Whole Child Community Conversations Project* (www.ascd.org/communityconversations).

HOW TO USE THIS TOOL

Your Whole Child strategic planning team is encouraged to engage stakeholders in its work using the Community Conversations process. Use this tool to introduce the key elements of this process to team members. How will your team take advantage of this process to address its mission, long-range goals, annual performance indicators, and action planning priorities? Consider the key elements presented in this tool as a design template for informing your work.

TIPS AND VARIATIONS

- ✓ Collaborate with key stakeholders to design and implement your Community Conversation. Determine how your work will support your team's action plan as well as complement your school improvement or district strategic planning process.
- ✓ Consider having multiple Community Conversations with a variety of stakeholder groups throughout your region or district. Examine how results produce similar conclusions—as well as areas in which there may be disagreement or lack of consensus.
- ✓ Use the results of your Community Conversations to develop and articulate your long-term vision for your Whole Child Initiative.

www. ascd.org/communityconversations

Engaging Stakeholders Through Community Conversations—Where Are We? Where Do We Need to Go?

WHAT IS A WHOLE CHILD COMMUNITY CONVERSATION?

Where do students, parents, educators, community advocates, and business leaders stand on the issues and priorities articulated in the Whole Child Compact? How can community-wide organizations and businesses help public schools achieve these goals? Can we agree on a basic set of principles regarding how we educate our community's children?

To help answer these questions and inspire conversations, ASCD has launched the Whole Child Community Conversations Project, which will allow local communities to explore how to work together to support the whole child. Some communities may choose a more formal, community-wide event, while others may prefer smaller discussion groups.

For more detailed information about the Whole Child Community Conversations Project or helpful tools for conversations, visit www.ascd.org/wholechild.

MEASURES OF SUCCESS FOR THE WHOLE CHILD COMMUNITY CONVERSATIONS PROJECT INCLUDE

- Increased understanding among local stakeholders about the Whole Child approach to learning
- Better decision making that is informed by community input and that leads to a more comprehensive approach to learning for children
- Shared commitment to pursue recommendations from the Community Conversations that focus on a Whole Child approach to learning

Support from ASCD: An ASCD representative is available to answer any questions and is eager to learn more about the issues that arose in your conversations. Please contact wholechild@ascd.org with questions or for additional help and to share your findings.

INFORMATION FROM YOUR DISCUSSION WILL BE USED TO HELP

- Drive changes in policy and practice to expand the Whole Child approach to learning in schools and communities.
- Create a shared sense of responsibility for implementing an action plan for change that extends from the classroom into the community.
- Inform future public engagement efforts.
- Provide insights for a public report of findings to be disseminated nationally. The report will analyze and synthesize findings from communities participating in the project and offer guidance on next steps.

WHOLE CHILD COMMUNITY CONVERSATIONS PLANNING NOTES

1. Suggested Community Conversations planning team members:

2. Suggested stakeholders (individuals and groups) for our Community Conversation(s):

3. Suggested locations:

4. Suggested facilitator(s) and recorder(s):

5. Suggested focus questions:

6. Suggested action steps (including time line):

7. We will need to revisit or address the following logistical and organizational issues:

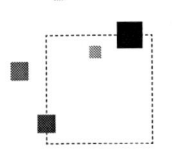

Action Tool Six: Creating and Sharing Your Vision for Education to Prepare Each Child for the 21st Century

PURPOSE OF THIS TOOL

By this point, your Whole Child strategic planning team should have an operational mission, guiding principles, preliminary action plan, and data from its Community Conversations. This tool is designed to help you extend and refine your collaborative work through the formulation of a vision for the long-range outcomes of your Whole Child strategic planning process. A mission typically describes operating principles that form a statement of purpose for your work. In contrast, a vision articulates your desired long-range impact statements: How will each student be affected by your work? How will your school or district affect the well-being and progress of each learner it serves?

HOW TO USE THIS TOOL

You can use this tool internally to guide initial discussion among your team members. They can use this tool's resources to generate a variety of potential vision statements for your Whole Child Initiative. Subsequently, a similar process can be replicated with other stakeholders and stakeholder groups. Ultimately, a collaborative vision should emerge that can function as a declaration of long-range impact statements that will unify all Whole Child activities and interventions.

TIPS AND VARIATIONS

- ✓ Use the results of implementing strategies from this tool to revisit your school or district's vision and mission statements. To what extent do they reflect the key elements of your Whole Child vision statement?
- ✓ Periodically revisit your Whole Child vision statement with team members and other stakeholders. Use it as a mirror for reflecting on the power, impact, and results of your Whole Child activities and interventions.
- ✓ Publish your Whole Child vision statement as part of your school or district Web site, newsletters, and related print and nonprint materials.

Overview

Creating and Sharing Your Vision for Education to Prepare Each Child for the 21st Century

CREATING A VISION FOR EDUCATION TO PREPARE EACH CHILD FOR THE 21ST CENTURY

Directions: Use the following quotes from *The Learning Compact Redefined: A Call to Action* to begin your vision-setting process. Which quotes resonate with members of your team or Community Conversation groups? Are there ideas in each quote that you might incorporate into your emerging Whole Child vision statement?

1. "There can be no keener revelation of a society's soul than the way in which it treats its children."

—Nelson Mandela

Key Ideas and Implications for Our Vision Statement:

2. "Children are the living message we send to a time we will not see."

—John W. Whitehead

Key Ideas and Implications for Our Vision Statement:

3. "Each moment we live never was before and will never be again. And yet what we teach children in school is 2 + 2 = 4 and Paris is the capital of France. What we should be teaching them is what they are. We should be saying, 'Do you know what you are? You are a marvel. You are unique. In all the world there is no other child exactly like you. In the millions of years that have passed, there has never been another child exactly like you. You may become a Shakespeare, a Michelangelo, a Beethoven. You have the capacity for anything. Yes, you are a marvel.'"

—Pablo Casals

Key Ideas and Implications for Our Vision Statement:

4. "We call on communities—educators, parents, businesses, health and social service providers, arts professionals, recreation leaders, and policy makers at all levels—to forge a new compact with our young people to ensure their whole and healthy development. We ask communities to redefine learning to focus on the whole person. We ask schools and communities to lay aside perennial battles for resources and instead align those resources in support of the whole child. Policy, practice, and resources must be aligned to support not only academic learning for each child, but also the experiences that encourage development of a whole child—one who is knowledgeable, healthy, motivated, and engaged."

—Stephanie Pace Marshall, Cochair, Commission on the Whole Child

Key Ideas and Implications for Our Vision Statement:

5. "To the doctor, the child is a typhoid patient; to the playground supervisor, a first baseman; to the teacher, a learner of arithmetic. At times, he may be different things to each of these specialists, but too rarely is he a whole child to any of them."

—From the 1930 report of the White House Conference on Children and Youth

Action Tool Six: Creating and Sharing Your Vision for Education to Prepare Each Child for the 21st Century

Key Ideas and Implications for Our Vision Statement:

6. "Institutions that support the whole child . . . must be both very structured and very free. There must be a sense of consistency and mindfulness in every detail of the space, from the schedule to . . . the tone of personal interactions to the system of expectations. . . . But there must also be flexibility and looseness, the possibility for creativity and spontaneity."

—Kate Quarfordt, Director, Artistic Program, Bronx Preparatory School

Key Ideas and Implications for Our Vision Statement:

A VISION PLANNING TEMPLATE

Directions: Based on feedback from the key ideas vision-setting activities, develop suggested vision statements for the Whole Child tenets and related elements.

Tenet	A Suggested Vision Statement for This Tenet
1. Each student enters school healthy and learns about and practices a healthy lifestyle.	
2. Each student learns in an intellectually challenging environment that is physically and emotionally safe for students and adults.	
3. Each student is actively engaged in learning and is connected to the school and broader community.	
4. Each student has access to personalized learning and to qualified, caring adults.	
5. Each graduate is prepared for success in college or further study and for employment in a global environment.	

DRAFTING YOUR WHOLE CHILD VISION STATEMENT

1. Our vision for each child in our (school/district) is that he or she will:

2. Our vision for each school in our district is that it will:

3. Our vision for our community is that it will:

4. Our vision for each teacher in our (school/district) is that he or she will:

Based upon these commitments, we would present our Whole Child vision in the following way:

RESOURCES FOR USE WITH CREATING AND SHARING YOUR VISION FOR THE WHOLE CHILD

We have included the following articles from ASCD's *Educational Leadership* to support you in your work with Whole Child vision development. You may elect to use them as part of an initial collaborative discussion and information process.

Richard Rothstein, Tamara Wilder, & Rebecca Jacobsen (2007, May). Balance in the balance. By strictly focusing on the academic basics, we fail to address the complex needs of 21st century learners.

Nel Noddings (2005, September). What does it mean to educate the whole child? A democratic society demands more of its schools than producing graduates proficient in reading and math.

Elliot Eisner (2005, September). Back to whole. The author looks at the dominating values guiding our current reform efforts.

Nel Noddings (2008, February). All our students thinking. Any subject promotes critical thinking if it is taught in intellectually challenging ways.

Richard Rothstein (2008, April). Whose problem is poverty? Modest social and economic reforms can greatly improve student achievement.

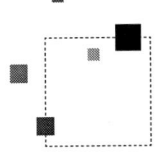

Action Tool Seven: Whole Child Professional Development Principles

PURPOSE OF THIS TOOL

A key component of your strategic planning process for your Whole Child Initiative will be developing and implementing a range of professional development processes that support your commitment to student achievement and organizational effectiveness. This tool synthesizes key principles and recommendations representative of current best practices in the field of professional development. These principles reinforce several key Whole Child tenets: (1) the need to involve and promote the development of all stakeholders; (2) the need to approach your work with the Whole Child process holistically, avoiding fragmentation and organizational isolation; (3) the critical need to ensure that your work is integrated into your overall school improvement planning process; and (4) the need to avoid one-shot, stand-and-deliver trainings in favor of job-embedded, inquiry-driven professional development that includes study groups, inquiry teams, and action research projects.

HOW TO USE THIS TOOL

This tool is designed as a catalyst for self-reflection and planning. Each member of your Whole Child strategic planning team should complete the questionnaire independently. Then team members should compare their results and arrive at consensus about the current status of organizational approaches to Whole Child professional development. Once you have reached agreement about current conditions, use the principles and recommendations in this questionnaire as a springboard for planning initial and long-term professional development activities to support your Whole Child long-range goals and annual performance targets.

TIPS AND VARIATIONS

- ✓ Revisit the principles and ideas presented in this tool as you work with each of the sections in this ASCD action tool addressing individual Whole Child tenets.
- ✓ Incorporate suggestions from this tool into the evaluation components of your Whole Child strategic plan, revisiting the issue of the value-added impact of your professional development programs and activities.
- ✓ Align your professional development activities for the Whole Child with other aspects of your school improvement planning process. Continue to ensure that your professional development processes are aligned with your total strategic plan for your organization.

Whole Child Professional Development Principles

DIRECTIONS:

1. Have each of your Whole Child strategic planning team members complete this questionnaire independently. Rate each item using the following scale: 4 = Highly evident and consistent in all areas; 3 = Evident but needs improvement in some areas; 2 = Evident in a few areas but needs overall improvement and greater emphasis; 1 = Minimally present and needs extensive attention and improvement; 0 = Absent.
2. During a team meeting, compare your individual responses and calculate averages.
3. Discuss what these emerging data patterns suggest about your current Whole Child professional development practices. For example, in what areas are you all in agreement? Are there areas about which you disagree or have differing perceptions?
4. Conclude your meeting by synthesizing what your results suggest about immediate and long-range professional development needs for your Whole Child strategic planning process.

Suggested Whole Child Professional Development Principle	Rating (4–0)
1. Our professional development involves all relevant stakeholders.	4 3 2 1 0
2. Our professional development is job embedded, ensuring that the needs and developmental priorities of our stakeholders are addressed effectively.	4 3 2 1 0
3. We avoid one-shot, stand-and-deliver experiences in favor of collaborative and inquiry-based professional development that puts the adult learner at the center of his or her own development.	4 3 2 1 0
4. We design our professional development based on careful feedback data aligned with our school improvement plan priorities, including our long-range goals and annual performance targets.	4 3 2 1 0
5. We are sensitive to the needs of the adult learner, ensuring that all participants understand the purpose of what they are doing, why they are being asked to do it, and how it supports their professional growth.	4 3 2 1 0
6. We determine the value added of all professional development activities, ensuring that we identify correlations between those activities and changes in participants' professional behavior and student achievement.	4 3 2 1 0
7. Our professional development is long range in its design, revisiting key knowledge, understandings, and skills through follow-up sessions and activities.	4 3 2 1 0
8. Whenever possible, we empower staff members to design and conduct professional development activities, reinforcing the concepts of distributed leadership and job-embedded learning.	4 3 2 1 0
9. We design collaborative introductory professional development sessions that enable participants to acquire a baseline knowledge and understanding of key principles and big ideas.	4 3 2 1 0
10. We follow up introductory sessions with opportunities for interested stakeholders to engage in study group sessions to extend and deepen their understanding.	4 3 2 1 0
11. We use inquiry team activities to extend study group work into collaborative decision-making and problem-solving sessions to help focus our work with one or more Whole Child priorities.	4 3 2 1 0

Suggested Whole Child Professional Development Principle (continued)	Rating (4–0)
12. We design and implement action research projects that help us to identify and replicate best practices related to one or more of our Whole Child long-range goals and annual performance target areas.	4 3 2 1 0
13. We incorporate lesson study opportunities to reinforce staff members' opportunities for peer coaching and feedback.	4 3 2 1 0
14. We provide learning opportunities for stakeholder groups such as parents, families, community, government, and business representatives.	4 3 2 1 0
15. We ensure that we integrate our Whole Child priorities in professional development programs and activities.	4 3 2 1 0
16. We offer professional development related to ensuring that our school reflects the characteristics of a healthy organization.	4 3 2 1 0
17. We offer professional development designed to help each educator model healthy practices related to healthy lifestyles.	4 3 2 1 0
18. We offer professional development to ensure that our teachers and administrators can help each student understand and practice healthy behaviors.	4 3 2 1 0
19. Our professional development related to instructional practices helps each staff member promote engaging and intellectually challenging learning environments for every student.	4 3 2 1 0
20. Our professional development specifically reinforces the need to ensure that every learning environment is both physically and emotionally healthy for all participants.	4 3 2 1 0
21. Our professional development ensures that every educator personalizes the learning environment for each student he or she teaches.	4 3 2 1 0
22. Because of our professional development, every student works with qualified and caring adults.	4 3 2 1 0
23. Our professional development reinforces strategies and practices designed to help each student master 21st century workplace competencies (e.g., problem solving, decision making, critical reasoning, technology competency, communication skills, team-based interaction skills).	4 3 2 1 0
24. We monitor and adjust our professional development practices to ensure that all stakeholder needs are met successfully.	4 3 2 1 0
25. We use a longitudinal process of program evaluation to ensure that our professional development meets the specific needs of all our stakeholders.	4 3 2 1 0
26. We provide the time and related resources to ensure that we maximize the impact of our professional development activities.	4 3 2 1 0

CONSENSUS BUILDING:

1. In what areas of this questionnaire do we have the greatest level of agreement?

2. How do we interpret the data results for those areas in which we agree? For example, what do the data suggest about the quality of our current professional development related to key aspects of the Whole Child strategic planning process?

3. Are there areas about which we disagree? How can we achieve consensus about those areas?

4. Based upon our initial discussion, what recommendations can we make about future professional development related to our Whole Child strategic planning process?

5. What action steps can we take to incorporate our conclusions into our Whole Child strategic plan?

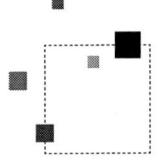

Action Tool Eight: Whole Child Study Group

PURPOSE OF THIS TOOL

This tool establishes a protocol for using study groups methodology as part of your Whole Child professional development process. Study groups are an essential component of sustained professional inquiry. They empower stakeholders to develop sufficient knowledge, skills, and understanding about Whole Child practices.

HOW TO USE THIS TOOL

This tool will help participants engage in dialogue and conduct gap analysis activities related to the major goals of the Whole Child strategic plan.

TIPS AND VARIATIONS

- ✓ Use this tool to extend and refine staff members' understanding of the study group process and its potential contributions to your school or district's work with the total Whole Child Initiative. A variety of study group activities can be used to establish a professional development infrastructure for your school. Specific components for discussion and analysis include the following:
  - The rationale for use of study groups within your professional development program
  - The potential purposes of study groups to support your Whole Child Initiative
  - Strategies for getting started with study groups in your school or district
  - Establishing a schedule and group norms for study group work
  - Creating an action plan for study groups in your school or district
  - Dealing with leadership and group facilitation issues
  - Selecting content for study group activities
  - Overcoming inevitable challenges associated with study group work
- ✓ At the completion of initial discussion of the implications of Whole Child study group work, provide time and resources for inquiry team activities. Inquiry teams can formulate action plans to address tenet-based student issues and organizational performance gaps. At the completion of inquiry team activities, you may wish to investigate the use of action research activities and processes to address identified problems and make decisions.

Whole Child Study Group

WHAT IS A STUDY GROUP? HOW CAN YOU USE STUDY GROUPS RELATED TO YOUR WORK WITH THE FIVE WHOLE CHILD TENETS?

1. A study group is composed of people who gather together to examine a predetermined topic. Professional development educators often form study groups out of a recognized need or interest or in recognition of the importance of constantly improving their own learning.
2. Study groups provide participants with a forum for learning together, planning together, testing ideas together, and reflecting together. For purposes of the five Whole Child tenets, participants will investigate research and selected readings related to the key elements of each tenet identified in their Whole Child strategic plan or school improvement plan.
3. Study groups can serve a variety of purposes, including helping participants to (1) learn about research-based best practices for each tenet, (2) identify potential performance gaps in tenet-related focus areas, (3) enhance the quality of their strategic plan or school improvement plan's attention to key tenet-related goals, and (4) prepare the way for developing and implementing inquiry group and action research projects to support the school's ability to address identified problems and performance targets.
4. Typically, a professional study group should include no more than six people. The smaller the group, the more each member will participate and take responsibility. Members of a study group should have common interests and needs, as well as an expressed commitment to improving the capacity of students to achieve goals associated with each of the Whole Child tenets.

WHAT ARE THE KEY STEPS IN FORMING AND CONDUCTING STUDY GROUPS FOR THE FIVE WHOLE CHILD TENETS?

1. **Scheduling Your Study Group Meetings:** After your study group is formed, set up a regular schedule of meetings—and agree to keep that schedule. Protect the time from other intrusions and reinforce the importance of your study group's activities. Decide on a schedule. Study groups usually meet every week or two for one or two hours. Also, be sure to set the times and days of your meetings as far in advance as possible and for as much time as you think you will need to address your tenet-related topics.
2. **Establishing Meeting Locations:** Choose a meeting site and make arrangements to secure the site over an extended period. If your group includes members from several different locations, you may decide to rotate locations of meetings.
3. **Establishing Group Norms:** Collectively agree on what is acceptable behavior in group settings. Reach consensus on such issues as the following:

- Beginning and ending the meeting on time
- Taking responsibility for one's own learning
- Practicing active participation
- Keeping what is said in the group within the group
- Respecting others' opinions
- Completing assignments

- Being open to change
- Practicing active listening
- Strategies for reminding one another when a norm is not being respected (e.g., posting a chart of consensus-driven norms for each meeting)

4. **Creating an Action Plan:** Each study group working on Whole Child tenets and performance issues should develop an individual action plan. The group should determine how the team will go about conducting its investigation. Such a plan will help participants stay on task, plan ahead, and keep focused on their goal(s). The plan should not be a detailed schedule of activities but a broad framework that the group can refer to as it progresses. Your study group action plan might include the following:

   - **Problem Identification:** State one or more problems identified with the tenet or tenets you wish to explore.
   - **Intended Results for Participants:** Members will learn about and implement strategies related to your identified goal(s). Discussions should center on both group and individual goals for participation in the tenet-related study group process.
   - **Intended Results for Students:** If appropriate, your study group may identify specific results for students, either as a whole within the school or as individuals and groups of students within one or more participants' classrooms.
   - **Study Group Time Line:** Ensure that each member agrees to the number of study group meetings, locations, and related logistics for each session.
   - **Resources:** This action tool provides *Educational Leadership* articles in electronic format that can serve as a beginning set of resources for study group discussions.

5. **Identifying Group Leadership:** Leadership in a study group can take a variety of forms. At your first meeting, for instance, establish who is going to take the leadership role and whether this person will remain the leader throughout the study period. It is often useful to establish a rotating schedule for study group leadership so that each member serves as a leader during the study process. Shared leadership makes everyone responsible for the success of the group and prompts individual group members to look to themselves and one another for direction. Leadership may rotate weekly, biweekly, or monthly. The leader for the group is responsible for (1) confirming logistics, (2) gathering any materials the group needs, (3) calling the meeting to order, and (4) reinforcing norms for shared accountability.

6. **Distributing Roles During a Study Group Session:** It is especially important for study group members to distribute leadership, where appropriate. To support this process, consider using a range of assigned tasks and roles for group members. You may wish to use task or role cards at each meeting to ensure that all participants have the opportunity to contribute in a variety of ways to group activities. Tasks and roles might include the following (note that each member may fill more than one role):

   - **Facilitator:** Ensures that everyone contributes and keeps the group on task.
   - **Recorder:** Keeps notes on important thoughts, ideas, and recommendations expressed in the group. Writes the final summary.
   - **Reporter:** Shares summary of study group meetings with larger groups (e.g., at faculty meetings). Speaks for the group, not from just a personal point of view.
   - **Materials Manager:** Collects, distributes, and puts away materials. Manages materials during group work.

- **Timekeeper:** Keeps track of the time during the meeting and reminds the group of how much time is left.
- **Checker:** Checks for accuracy and clarity of thinking during discussions. May also verify records of meetings.
- **Additional Goal-Oriented Task Roles:** Additional roles that support the achievement of meeting goals include initiator, information seeker, informer, clarifier, summarizer, and reality tester.
- **Additional Interaction-Oriented Task Roles:** Addition roles that support positive group dynamics include harmonizer, gatekeeper, consensus taker, encourager, and compromiser.

7. **Strategies for Building Consensus and Promoting Positive Interactions:** Several universal strategies can promote positive group dynamics and consensus building within a study group. These include tokens (e.g., giving each member five tokens and, once they have been used, the participant refrains from speaking until all members have used their tokens) and dot consensus (e.g., a voting strategy in which all ideas are listed on large sheets of paper and participants use 5 to 10 colored dots to express their support of one or more of the ideas, with the most popular receiving further analysis or implementation status).

8. **Bringing Closure to Study Group Activities:** A study group is in control of its own longevity. Each study group should decide when its goals have been accomplished and how long it should continue to meet. At the beginning of your study group process, you should commit to a specific number of meetings, with consideration of extensions as you work. Additionally, your study group needs to determine how it will share its observations, conclusions, and recommendations with the rest of the faculty as it progresses and as it concludes its work.

Adapted from R. Marzano & T. Guskey (developers) (2002). *ASCD professional inquiry kit, Grading and reporting student learning professional inquiry kit.* Alexandria, VA: Association for Supervision and Curriculum Development.

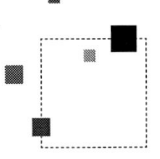

Action Tool Nine: Inquiry Teams and Whole Child Problem-Solving and Decision-Making Processes

PURPOSE OF THIS TOOL

As study groups complete their initial work, they can expand their efforts into the realm of inquiry team activities. Inquiry teams can be used to identify major problems and decisions that will need to be addressed to achieve your Whole Child goals and annual performance targets. They are a logical transition point for moving staff members from initial study group activities into the more complex and challenging work of collaborative action research.

HOW TO USE THIS TOOL

After one or more study groups have completed their initial analysis, discussion, and investigation of key issues and research-based practices related to Whole Child tenets and related improvement processes, interested participants can be supported to form inquiry teams using the resources in this section. This tool provides an introductory framework for inquiry teamwork, including suggestions for formulating focus questions related to key Whole Child problems and decisions. There is also a planning template that articulates key elements of recommended Whole Child problem-solving and decision-making processes.

TIPS AND VARIATIONS

- ✓ Inquiry teams should be viewed as relatively brief in duration. In effect, they should become the springboard or catalyst for developing collaborative action research projects focusing upon gaps and achievement issues in key Tenet One areas.
- ✓ Study groups may wish to use inquiry team methodology to bring closure to their work. After a majority of study group members perceive themselves as having sufficient knowledge and understanding of key Whole Child tenets, they can examine current organizational practices and identify areas of omission, gaps, and weakness in need of attention and focus as part of the strategic planning process.
- ✓ After identifying organizational areas of need related to Whole Child tenets, inquiry team participants can collaborate on identifying an action research project they are interested in pursuing.
- ✓ Inquiry teams can also be effective ways for school improvement teams to investigate achievement and organizational productivity issues related to the Whole Child tenets. As a result of an inquiry team's work, a school improvement plan can be enhanced using feedback and recommendations from the inquiry team.

Inquiry Teams and Whole Child Problem-Solving and Decision-Making Processes

Part I: Possible Whole Child Inquiry Team Investigation Questions

1. What barriers and issues do we need to address to help each student enter school healthy?
2. How can we improve collaboration with schools in our feeder pattern to better help each student enter school healthy?
3. What are the barriers and issues we face in terms of making our school a healthy one?
4. What impedes families in our community from accessing needed health and human services? What decisions will we need to make to address these problems?
5. What problems are evident currently among individual students, subgroups of students, and our aggregate student body in terms of their choices about healthy behavior?
6. To what extent are health, nutrition, and physical fitness issues evident among our students?
7. To what extent are health, nutrition, and physical fitness issues evident among our staff members?
8. What problems exist in our staff members' understanding of how to model healthy choices and healthy lifestyles for our students?
9. What problems and impediments keep each of our students from experiencing their education as intellectually challenging?
10. How can we refine our ability to promote intellectual challenge for each of our students?
11. What problems exist in our school or district that detract from our learning environment being physically safe for all participants?
12. What problems exist in our school or district that detract from our learning environment being emotionally safe for all participants?
13. What barriers and issues keep each of our students from feeling engaged in their learning process?
14. What keeps students in our school or district from feeling connected to our school(s) and the learning environments they provide?
15. What obstructs our ability to personalize the learning environment of each of our students?
16. What issues and problems exist with our recruiting process for hiring new teachers?
17. What issues and problems exist with ensuring that each of our students works with qualified, caring adults?
18. What decisions are needed to improve our long-term professional development for our staff to ensure that each student works with qualified, caring adults?
19. What feedback do we get from employers in our community about the quality of our graduates who work for them? How can we address identified problems and deficiencies in this area?
20. How successful are our students when they participate in postsecondary education (e.g., college, university, vocational school, military training)? What problems and gaps do we need to address in this area?
21. To what extent do our students graduate with competency in 21st century workplace skills and proficiencies? How do we know? What do we need to do to improve our understanding in this area?

WHOLE CHILD STRATEGIC PLANNING TEAM REACTIONS

1. What do we agree to be our most pressing problems in these identified areas?
2. What decisions will we need to make to address these problems?
3. What preliminary recommendations can we make for identified problems and decisions?

Part II: An Inquiry Team Planning Template

DIRECTIONS:

Use the planning guide to focus your inquiry team's efforts and to identify and implement action steps to address Whole Child issues or problems. This process can then guide your inquiry team in the action research process.

Inquiry Team Action Step	Questions and Recommendations for Each Step	Recommended Resources for Each Step
1. Identify the issue or question you wish to investigate (i.e., a potential gap between the ideal and the reality of current practice).		
2. Collect potential data sources related to your issue or question.		
3. Identify areas in which data sources are unavailable or insufficient to study the issue or question adequately.		
4. Analyze available data to discover aggregate and disaggregated patterns and conclusions.		
5. Develop and implement additional ways to collect and analyze data.		

Inquiry Team Action Step	Questions and Recommendations for Each Step	Recommended Resources for Each Step
6. Begin to draw inferences and evaluate the status of the issue or question you have investigated: (a) What are current strengths associated with our existing programs or practices? (b) What are current problems and barriers that need to be addressed?		
7. Based on your data analysis process, identify practices and policies to address problems and barriers.		
8. As your inquiry team progresses, use resources from your study group activities to identify research-based best practices associated with your identified issue, problem, or decision.		
9. When your inquiry team members feel ready to suggest solutions to the identified issue, problem, or decision, develop your action plan, for example, projected outcomes, suggested solutions, time line, resources, participants, suggested evaluation strategies.		
10. After your inquiry team completes its recommended action plan, present it to relevant stakeholders for input and modification.		
11. Use your action plan as a springboard for action research.		

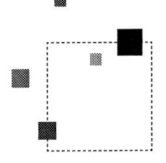

Action Tool Ten: The Whole Child Action Research Process

PURPOSE OF THIS TOOL

The job-embedded professional development model recommended for your Whole Child planning process emphasizes the power of collaborative inquiry. This process involves staff members moving from initial study group investigations toward focusing their inquiry teamwork on identifying unresolved Whole Child issues and priorities. Next, they should engage in focused action research to develop and implement an action plan to address one or more problems, issues, and concerns related to the five Whole Child tenets. This tool provides an overview of action research questions for your Whole Child planning process and a set of action research planning steps to guide the process.

HOW TO USE THIS TOOL

Begin by having your Whole Child planning team consider the action research questions; then determine if any of them seem relevant or important for your work. You might adopt one of the research questions as written or adapt it for your particular needs. Use the accompanying planning template to establish action research teams.

TIPS AND VARIATIONS

- ✓ Consider having several action research projects occur simultaneously. Compare conclusions and results throughout the academic year.
- ✓ Explore ways to expand and replicate the use of practices and policies confirmed by the action research process to have a positive impact on students, community members, staff, or organizational productivity.
- ✓ Investigate ways to use the action research process to guide and inform the decisions you make and approaches you take toward community involvement and engagement.

The Whole Child Action Research Process

Part I: Action Research Questions for the Five Whole Child Tenets

1. How can we ensure that each student enters school healthy?
2. How can we ensure that each student learns about and practices a healthy lifestyle?
3. How can we ensure that each staff member is equipped to help students understand and practice healthy behaviors?
4. How can we collaborate to ensure that our school reflects the characteristics of a healthy learning organization?
5. How can we help each student learn in an intellectually challenging environment?
6. How can we ensure that our school is physically healthy and safe for every student and adult in our learning community?
7. How can we ensure that our school is emotionally safe for every student and adult in our learning community?
8. How can we ensure that each student is actively engaged in learning?
9. How can we ensure that each student feels connected to our school?
10. How can we help each student to feel connected to his or her community?
11. How can we personalize the learning environment for every student?
12. How can we ensure that every student works with qualified, caring adults?
13. How can we prepare each graduate for success in a college or other postsecondary learning institution?
14. How can we prepare each graduate for successful employment in a global environment?

Part II: Whole Child Action Research Process Checklist

- Identify members of the action research team for the tenet(s) you intend to investigate.
- Identify a tenet-related student achievement issue or organizational productivity problem you would like to investigate.
- Collect and analyze available data related to the issue or problem for the tenet(s). Present your initial conclusions and analyses to key stakeholders.
- Based on your initial data analysis and presentation process, create an action research hypothesis you intend to investigate.
- Reformulate your hypothesis as an action research question that will guide your research process.
- Based on your action research question, develop an initial tenet-related action plan to inform your research investigation (e.g., identified interventions, time line, research cadre, evaluation processes, methods for presenting your conclusions).
- Implement your tenet-related action plan, studying the impact of identified interventions and strategies upon the performance targets you are studying.
- At key junctures in your action research process, formulate tenet-related conclusions and analyze data patterns.
- Share your tenet-related conclusions, insights, and observations with other staff members and community stakeholders. Explore opportunities for expanding and replicating staff use of interventions proven to make a difference in student achievement.
- Make appropriate modifications to your tenet-related action plan as new data become available.
- Incorporate successful tenet-based practices resulting from your action research process into your existing school improvement plan or Whole Child strategic plan.

Part III: Ballot for Choosing Action Research Questions

Directions: Action research questions should stimulate curiosity and focus your implementation of practices. The facilitator or small groups should select four questions that may be of interest to group members and that are aligned with the issues and goals of your school community. Have participants rate their reaction to the questions. Votes should be tallied and then reported to the larger group to determine action research work.

QUESTION 1:

When I think about this question, I am

| Not excited | Not sure | Mildly curious | Very curious | Have ideas about answer | Already know answer |

QUESTION 2:

When I think about this question, I am

| Not excited | Not sure | Mildly curious | Very curious | Have ideas about answer | Already know answer |

QUESTION 3:

When I think about this question, I am

| Not excited | Not sure | Mildly curious | Very curious | Have ideas about answer | Already know answer |

QUESTION 4:

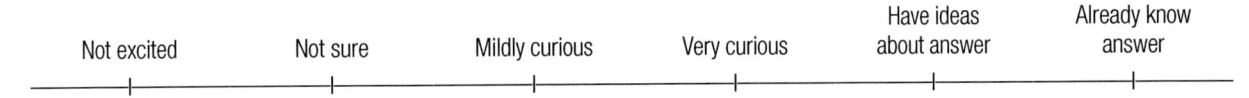

When I think about this question, I am

| Not excited | Not sure | Mildly curious | Very curious | Have ideas about answer | Already know answer |

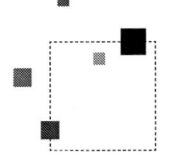

Action Tool Eleven: Key Elements of the Whole Child Strategic Planning Process

PURPOSE OF THIS TOOL

This tool provides a model for two interrelated approaches to designing your Whole Child plan: (1) incorporating your Whole Child conclusions, processes, and implementation strategies into your existing school improvement plan or (2) developing a stand-alone Whole Child strategic plan (if you determine the need to emphasize key Whole Child components independently). This tool can be used to guide your planning team's recommendations for addressing key Whole Child focus areas. Also, in the "Putting It All Together" section of this guide, you will find a sample completed strategic plan synthesizing several of the tenets and related strategic planning elements.

HOW TO USE THIS TOOL

Use this tool to focus your work with all aspects of strategic planning for your overall Whole Child Initiative. It can become a framework and catalyst for helping you to (1) create your vision for each tenet; (2) develop goals and annual performance targets for each tenet; (3) identify, collect, and analyze relevant data sources; (4) generate an action plan for addressing identified priorities; (5) identify key elements of your professional development plan for the Whole Child; (6) delineate community outreach and engagement activities for follow-up; and (7) explore cross-tenet alignment and interconnections.

TIPS AND VARIATIONS

- ✓ Use this tool to ensure that Whole Child focus areas are infused into your existing school improvement plan. This process will ensure that the goals associated with each Whole Child tenet are an active part of your long-range planning process. It will also ensure that you monitor and evaluate the impact of identified practices and policies on student achievement and changes in the community and the organization.
- ✓ Be certain to share your initial draft of the plan with key stakeholders, incorporating their recommendations and additions into your final plan.

The Whole Child Action Research Project

WHOLE CHILD STRATEGIC PLANNING TEMPLATE

Whole Child Vision Statement:

Tenet Focus Areas:

Long-Range Goals	Performance Targets	Short-Term Goals	Performance Targets

WHOLE CHILD STRATEGIC PLANNING TEMPLATE (continued)

Whole Child Vision Statement:

Tenet Focus Areas:

Impact Data Sources	Time Line	Responsible Person/Group

WHOLE CHILD STRATEGIC PLANNING TEMPLATE (continued)

Whole Child Vision Statement:

Tenet Focus Areas:

Professional Development Activities	Stakeholder Outreach and Engagement Actions	Cross-Tenet Alignment	Supporting Projects/Other

WHOLE CHILD STRATEGIC PLANNING CONSIDERATIONS

- Goals can be focused on students, staff, parents/guardians, and the community.
- Performance targets should be measurable and observable and include value-added components.
- Suggestions should be included for ways the plan can support stakeholders in making connections among Whole Child tenets.
- Professional development plans should be developed in conjunction with the strategic plan and should address projected costs, necessary time and other resources, and gathering impact evidence.
- Student involvement and voice should be included in planning and implementation.

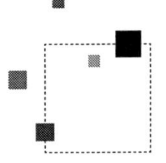

Action Tool Twelve: Sustaining Community Support and Collaboration

PURPOSE OF THIS TOOL

One of the most important aspects of successful Whole Child implementation initiatives is sustained community support and collaboration. This tool is designed to guide and support your planning for implementing ideas and suggestions. The examples listed are intended as a starting point for your work.

HOW TO USE THIS TOOL

Consider options for community support and cross-institutional partnerships. After investigating and discussing ideas, use the planning template to finalize your Whole Child team's recommendations for outreach and sustained stakeholder support.

TIPS AND VARIATIONS

✓ Have small groups work together on the planning tool. Share ideas with the larger group and come to consensus on implementation steps.

✓ Have stakeholder groups representing each category add new ideas and examples for outreach and suggestions for moving forward.

Sustaining Community Support and Collaboration

Use this tool in community and staff meetings to inform your Whole Child plan development and determine ideas for implementation.

Tenet:		
Focus Area	**Suggestions and Recommendations**	**Individuals Responsible**
1. Parenting		
2. Communicating		
3. Volunteering		
4. Learning at Home		
5. Decision Making		
6. Collaborating with the Community		
Other Stakeholder Partnerships and Collaborations		
7. College, University, and Other School Partnerships		
8. Business/Corporate Partnerships		
9. Service Organization Partnerships		
10. Career Awareness Activities		
11. Shadowing Experiences		
12. Mentorships		
13. Internships		
14. Externships		

Action Tool Twelve: Sustaining Community Support and Collaboration

Tenet:		
Focus Area	Suggestions and Recommendations	Individuals Responsible
15. Concurrent Enrollment		
16. Field Experiences for Academic Enrichment		
17. Tutoring		
18. Health and Human Services Collaboration		
19. Service Learning Organizations		
20. Multi-Age Service Outreach Activities		
21. Cross-School Service Options		

Family Support and Involvement

EXAMPLES FOR SUSTAINING COMMUNITY SUPPORT AND COLLABORATION
TENET FOUR COMMUNITY OUTREACH EXAMPLES

Family Support and Involvement: In *School, family, and community partnerships: Your handbook for action,* 2nd edition (Thousand Oaks, CA: Corwin Press, 2002), Joyce Epstein presents a six-type model for school, family, and community partnerships. For this tenet, schools using Epstein's model might include the following goals:

- Parenting: Help families advocate for services to meet their children's individual needs, strengths, and interests, and strategize for their long-term success. Provide parenting classes on such topics as positive discipline, role modeling, and managing the home environment to support child development. Educate families on how to select good out-of-school-time programs. Help families to monitor child-adult relationships both within the school and beyond it to ensure their child's engagement with qualified, caring adults.
- Communicating: Communicate to families a variety of student learning opportunities and options and ensure family understanding of available services (e.g., special education, gifted education, service learning, work study). Facilitate the home-school communication process as well as the school-home communication process, all centering around the recommendations presented in this section. Honor the language of the students and families, and, when feasible,

translate communications into the home language. Utilize a variety of communication strategies to inform families of within-school and beyond-school opportunities for mentoring, coaching, and learning by qualified, caring adults. Provide opportunities for families to communicate their needs, concerns, and challenges.

- Volunteering: Provide and coordinate opportunities for family volunteering in each of the areas identified in this section (e.g., mentorship, service learning). Identify family members who could act as mentors or be able to provide out-of-school learning opportunities.
- Learning at Home: Work with families to ensure that home conditions support homework. Offer coaching and support to families so that they can support conditions for learning within the home and can help their children understand the connection between education and long-term success (e.g., Family Math Night; How Do I Do Homework with My Ninth Grader?; technology courses for families participating as a group—with door prizes such as discounted computers; planning course sequences from middle to high school to meet graduation requirements; and helping parents and families to understand course sequences from middle to high school, including how students' course selections affect their ability to enter successfully both post-secondary education and the world of work.).
- Decision Making: Ensure that families are involved in curricular, instruction, and governance decisions beyond fundraising and social activities. Assess family perceptions of school climate and engage families when appropriate in review of school staff qualifications. This process may include family representation on hiring panels. Family representatives should be on cross-tenet advisory committees. Consider offering a Leadership Academy for families related to this tenet (and others). Ensure family representation on all Whole Child advisory committees and teams. Family members can play active roles in Parent Teacher Student Associations.
- Collaborating with the Community: Ensure that community activities in the school are coordinated and supervised by qualified, caring adults. Identify community activists and engage them in relevant processes related to the Whole Child Initiative in your school or district. Ensure that services are open to the community (e.g., Open Gym Night; library resources available to all family and community members).

College/University/School Partnerships: Form partnerships with local postsecondary education institutions to help staff explore current research and instructional, assessment, and learning practices that promote personalized and differentiated learning. Such partnerships are especially important in promoting higher levels of teacher certification and recertification, ensuring that qualified and caring adults work with all students in the school or district.

Community Partnerships (Business/Corporate): Encourage local businesses and corporations to allow their workers to participate in a range of outreach activities, including serving as role models, mentors, tutors, or facilitators of career shadowing experiences.

Community Partnerships (Service Organizations): Expand the pool of service agencies within the community that are willing to work with high school students in a variety of situations and contexts, including field experiences, internships, and service learning projects.

Career Awareness Activities: Encourage community representatives to take an active role in the design and implementation of career awareness activities. These can range from in-class presentations to participation in Career Days.

Shadowing Experiences: Enlist community representatives to serve as role models during shadowing experiences in which high school students visit a community work site or related venue and follow the individual during a part of his or her professional day.

Mentorships: Involve community representatives in mentoring roles. Mentors meet regularly with one or more students (usually at the school site) and serve as role models who offer advice, support, and encouragement as students prepare for postsecondary education or work experiences.

Internships: Provide formal and structured on-site work experiences in which students collaborate with one or more on-site mentors and experience a range of activities related to a career pathway of interest to them. Generally, an internship is monitored by a school-based professional. Internships are often aligned with related high school programs.

Externships: Ensure that there are informal and structured on-site work experiences paralleling the structures and processes of an internship, but with the experience monitored by a professional affiliated with the sponsoring organization.

Concurrent Enrollment: Encourage a maximum number of students to earn college credit by completing courses at nearby postsecondary institutions. Options for consideration include allowing college credit courses to substitute for senior-level coursework (where feasible).

Field Experiences for Academic Enrichment: Collaborate with a range of community-based businesses, corporations, service agencies, and other sites (e.g., museums, nature centers) to develop and implement regularly scheduled activities that align with students' high school coursework.

Tutoring: Encourage community members to serve as tutors in areas in which they have expertise. Tutoring sessions can be held at the school during school hours, before and after school, or through other arrangements made by school personnel.

Health and Human Services Collaborations: Help schools to become full-service agencies by finding ways to bring health, counseling, and social service agency representatives to the school to work with students in need. This full-service approach ensures that students have easy access to needed services, including options for family outreach and counseling.

Service Learning Options: Encourage community members to work with the school to expand the range of service learning opportunities available to interested students. Ideally, service learning options reinforce students' sense of ethical citizenship and are aligned with key learning outcomes in the students' core curriculum. Service learning options might include, for example, activities involving nature conservancy, legal aid, or direct participation in local or state governments.

Multi-Age Service Outreach Activities: Collaborate with service agencies in the area to facilitate student participation in service learning activities involving younger and older individuals. High school students, for example, might become mentors to struggling or at-risk elementary school students. Similarly, they might serve a variety of roles in local retirement homes or senior citizen centers.

Cross-School Service Options: Reinforcing communication and collaboration across feeder pattern lines (e.g., elementary, middle, and high school feeder patterns) can enhance high school students' options for service learning. A high school drama class, for example, might present a series of one-act plays or excerpts to student audiences in local middle and elementary schools.

TENET ONE TOOLS

Entering School Healthy and Promoting Healthy Schools and Healthy Lifestyles

INTRODUCTION 67

TITLE OF TOOL

1. Orientation, Group Discussion, and Initial Activities Exploring Key Criteria Associated with Tenet One. 69

2. Examining Your School's Current Status for Tenet One—Suggested Strategies for Data Collection and Analysis 75

3–7: Planning and Implementing Professional Development for Tenet One 79

    3. A Suggested Agenda for Your Tenet One Professional Development Activities 80

    4. Identifying Key Players in Your Tenet One Strategic Planning Process 81

    5. Characteristics of a Healthy School 83

    6. Helping Each Student Enter School Healthy and Ready to Learn 85

    7. Helping Adults Practice and Model Healthy Behaviors for Students 88

8. Study Group Articles and Discussion Questions 89

9. Inquiry Team and Action Research Questions 91

Entering School Healthy and Promoting Healthy Schools and Healthy Lifestyles

Introduction

This section will help educators and community members to address three primary goals: (1) to ensure that each student enters school healthy, (2) to ensure that the school as a learning organization reflects research-based practices and principles that promote health for all, and (3) to ensure that each student understands and practices a healthy lifestyle. A foundation for Whole Child education, Tenet One involves collaboration among stakeholders to promote the physical, social, and emotional well-being of all stakeholders.

As stakeholders begin to consider this first tenet of the Whole Child Initiative, they may wish to review the ASCD publication *Creating a Healthy School Using the Healthy School Report Card: An ASCD Action Tool* (www.healthyschoolcommunities.org). It recommends that healthy schools do the following:

- Ensure that students, family members, and community members play an active and sustained role in helping schools to achieve these goals through participation on the school health council, school wellness team, or other team that forms a system for coordinating efforts, eliminating gaps and overlaps, expanding student access to health resources, and ensuring a high-quality, coordinated approach to promoting school health.
- Support health through compliance with comprehensive policies that address all aspects of a coordinated school health program.
- Collaborate to ensure that the school culture and climate strongly support and reinforce the health literacy, knowledge, attitudes, behaviors, and skills students learn through a high-quality, sequential, and developmentally appropriate health education curriculum.
- Promote a school culture and climate that strongly supports and reinforces the lifelong fitness knowledge, attitudes, behaviors, and skills students learn through a high-quality, sequential, and developmentally appropriate physical education curriculum.
- Support, promote, and reinforce healthy eating patterns and food safety for students, staff, and families.

- Ensure student access to primary prevention, intervention, and treatment of disease and medical disorders.
- Facilitate student access to primary prevention, intervention, and treatment of mental health and substance abuse problems. Students and staff should also have access to alternate discipline interventions.
- Ensure high-level job performance and healthy role models by supporting and facilitating the physical and mental health and well-being of all employees.

This section begins with an introduction to the major focus areas of Tenet One. It provides a wide range of action tools that reinforce initial action planning discussions, suggestions for preliminary data collection and analysis, research-based best practices, a comprehensive set of professional development activities and resources, suggestions for Tenet One focus areas for your school improvement plan, and recommendations for community engagement and outreach.

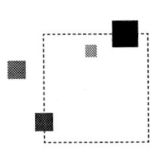

Action Tool One: Orientation, Group Discussion, and Initial Activities Exploring Key Criteria Associated with Tenet One

PURPOSE OF THIS TOOL

This tool introduces participants to the range of recommendations and processes to achieve the goals of helping students enter school healthy, promoting healthy school environments, and ensuring that students understand and practice healthy lifestyle choices.

HOW TO USE THIS TOOL

This tool offers a rich range of ideas and recommendations for your team's work with Tenet One. It can also be used to facilitate staff discussions concerning key elements of Tenet One. Whole Child strategic planning teams may also elect to use this tool for stakeholder discussions, including analyzing gaps and omissions in school health services, health education and physical education, and student access to health and human services. Perhaps most important, this tool can be used in a variety of venues to establish stakeholder consensus about the status of current Tenet One services and programs—and areas in which immediate and long-term work may need to occur.

TIPS AND VARIATIONS

- ✓ This tool can be used to support an initial study group. Use the materials and activities included here to focus members' understanding of the major structural components associated with successful Tenet One implementation.
- ✓ This tool can also be used with stakeholder conversations and strategic planning sessions dedicated to identifying priorities related to such issues as student health, nutrition, wellness, and physical fitness.
- ✓ Use these materials to investigate the issue of the emotional and physical well-being and health of the adults in your learning community. This focus can range from examining healthy practices and lifestyles among your staff members to ways in which your school may become a full-service learning community for families and community members.

Orientation, Group Discussion, and Initial Activities Exploring Key Criteria Associated with Tenet One

ACTIVITY—GALLERY WALK

- Post each of the gallery walk statements below around the room. Draw two columns on each page with the headings "Have in place" and "Add."
- Divide the participants into small groups.
- Ask each small group to indicate
  - What is in place in our school that supports the statement?
  - What do we need to add to make the statement true?
- Have each group rotate around and add any new ideas to the lists.
- Provide stick-on dots to participants. Have them select three items in the Add column to indicate their top three priority choices.
- Use the information for planning priorities.

1. As you begin your Tenet One strategic planning process, how would you describe the status of the major elements of this tenet as they operate in your school or district?

    1. Each of our students enters school healthy.
    2. Each of our schools reflects the characteristics of a healthy building and organization.
    3. Each of our staff members models and reinforces for students healthy choices and healthy lifestyles (including healthy eating, physical activity, health and well-being).
    4. Each of our students learns about healthy behaviors and lifelong health.
    5. Each of our students chooses healthy behaviors.
    6. Each of our students practices a healthy lifestyle.

ACTIVITY—DISCUSSION

Divide the group into pairs or small groups that include at least one person who is connected to the discussion area. Include others who are not specifically connected to the area. Assign each small group one or two elements of a coordinated approach to school health to read about and discuss.

Have each small group report its reactions and recommendations. Have all comments recorded to use in developing the plan.

2. Consider the status of each of the following in your school or district. For example, to what extent is each fully functional? To what extent is it easily accessible for each student and his or her family? How do staff members benefit from these resources and organizational practices?

A. **Health Education:** A planned, sequential, K–12 curriculum addresses the physical, mental, emotional, and social dimensions of health. The curriculum is designed to motivate and assist students to maintain and improve their health, prevent disease, and reduce health-related risky behaviors.

Reactions and Recommendations:

B. **Physical Education:** A planned, sequential K–12 curriculum provides cognitive content and learning experiences in a variety of activity areas and promotes each student's optimum physical, mental, emotional, and social development through a variety of planned physical activities. Successful contemporary physical education programs promote activities and sports that all students enjoy and can pursue throughout their lives.

Reactions and Recommendations:

C. **Health Services:** A Whole Child school or district provides easily accessed services designed to protect and promote student health. Qualified professionals such as physicians, nurses, dentists, health educators, and other allied health personnel provide these services. These services
- Ensure access or referral to primary health care services or both
- Foster appropriate use of primary health care services
- Prevent and control communicable disease and other health problems
- Provide emergency care for illness or injury
- Promote and provide optimum sanitary conditions for a safe school facility and school environment
- Provide educational and counseling opportunities for promoting and maintaining individual, family, and community health

Reactions and Recommendations:

D. **Nutrition Services:** A Whole Child school or district provides access to a variety of nutritious and appealing meals that accommodate the health and nutrition needs of all students. School nutrition programs should reflect appropriate nutrition standards identified by agencies or health organizations. School nutrition services offer students a learning laboratory for classroom nutrition and health education and serve as a resource for links with nutrition-related community services. Qualified child nutrition professionals should provide these services.

Reactions and Recommendations:

E. **Counseling and Psychological Services:** Services provided to improve students' mental, emotional, and social health include individual and group assessments, interventions, and referrals. Organizational assessment and consultation skills of counselors and psychologists contribute not only to the health of students but also to the health of the school environment. Professionals such as certified school counselors, psychologists, and social workers provide these services.

Reactions and Recommendations:

F. **Healthy School Environment:** The factors that influence the physical surroundings and operations of the school environment include the school building and the area surrounding it; any biological or chemical agents that are detrimental to health; and physical conditions such as temperature, noise, lighting, and the flow of people within that environment.

Reactions and Recommendations:

G. **Healthy School Environment:** Factors that influence the aesthetic surroundings and the psycho-social climate and culture of the school—what has been labeled "the psychological environment"—include the physical, emotional, and social conditions that affect the well-being of students and staff. Typically, they include the norms, mores, and standards articulated for human interactions within the environment—and the extent to which those standards are equitably applied to all participants within that environment.

Reactions and Recommendations:

H. **Health Promotion for Staff:** Opportunities for school staff to improve their health status include activities such as health assessments, health education, and health-related fitness activities. These opportunities encourage school staff to pursue a healthy lifestyle that contributes to improved health status, improved morale, and a greater personal commitment to the school's overall coordinated health program. This personal commitment often translates into greater commitment to the health of students and creates positive role modeling. Health promotion activities can improve productivity, decrease absenteeism, and reduce health insurance costs.

Reactions and Recommendations:

I. **Family/Community Involvement:** An integrated school, parent, and community approach enhances the health and well-being of students. School health advisory councils, coalitions, and broadly based constituencies for school health can build support for school health program efforts. Schools actively solicit parent involvement and engage community resources and services to respond more effectively to the health-related needs of students.

Reactions and Recommendations:

J. **Coordination:** The essential structures and activities are in place to facilitate coordination of all health programs to eliminate gaps and overlaps, expand access to health resources, and ensure high quality.

Reactions and Recommendations:

Adapted from www.cdc.gov/healthyyouth and David K. Lohrmann (2005). *Creating a Healthy School Using the Healthy School Report Card.* Alexandria, VA: Association for Supervision and Curriculum Development.

Tenet One Discussion Activity One: Processing Sheet
Based on our initial discussions of key Tenet One research-based practices, we commend our school(s) for the following successful Tenet One structures and services:
Based on our initial discussions of key Tenet One research-based practices, we have identified the following gaps or areas in need of greater attention and development:
We recommend that the following become immediate priorities for follow-up by our Whole Child team:

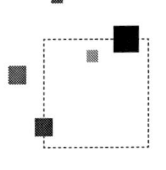

Action Tool Two: Examining Your School's Current Status for Tenet One—Suggested Strategies for Data Collection and Analysis

PURPOSE OF THIS TOOL

As your team completes its preliminary discussion and analysis of Tenet One programs and practices in your school or district, a logical next step is preliminary data collection and analysis related to your recommendations. This tool will provide a process and methodology for your team to begin determining how accurate your initial insights and recommendations were, based on available student, staff, and related stakeholder data.

HOW TO USE THIS TOOL

Examine the recommendations presented in this tool. Consider the available evidence to determine the extent to which each element or strategy is fully operational. For areas in which you have insufficient data to draw conclusions, consider how your team might acquire those data to make valid inferences and recommendations.

TIPS AND VARIATIONS

- ✓ Use this tool and the analytical processes it generates to determine key elements of your Tenet One work. For example, who will the key change agents be? Who needs to be involved to address Tenet One gaps and emerging priorities and goals? How will we involve students, parents, and the community?
- ✓ Be certain to communicate your conclusions and recommendations to members of your school improvement team as well as other stakeholders.
- ✓ The completion of the discussion and analysis process facilitated through Action Tool Two is an ideal time for your team to engage in outreach to individuals and organizations that can support your recommended changes. In addition to finding experts (e.g., university researchers, program directors, central office leaders) who can help you with your work, you will need to start the conversation: How will we sustain recommended organizational changes?

Examining Your School's Current Status for Tenet One—Suggested Strategies for Data Collection and Analysis

DIRECTIONS:

Activity—Trio Share

1. Form groups of three.
2. Distribute the data collection tool to each person and have them complete it individually.
3. In each trio, have participants reflect individually and then discuss the following as a group:
   - Explain the score on current status.
   - Discuss why the priority status score was selected.
4. Have each trio develop consensus for the five questions that follow the status assessment.

Now that you have begun identifying areas in which there may be need for more extensive emphasis on key practices in your school or district, answer the following three questions to build consensus about the statements in the table that follows:

1. What is the status of each of the following research-based best practices in your learning organization? (4 = Highly and consistently evident; 3 = Evident in some but not all relevant school operations; 2 = Operational but needs extensive attention and development; 1 = Minimally available for a majority of students, staff, and other stakeholders; 0 = Absent)
2. Which of the best practices do you consider high priority and in need of the greatest and most immediate attention to serve our students more effectively? (4 = Extremely important—should be an immediate priority; 3 = Important and should be addressed during this academic year; 2 = Important, but we can make this a priority later; 1 = We can attend to this in later phases of our strategic planning process; 0 = Very low priority)
3. What are the data sources and data collection processes you will need to engage in to confirm our conclusions?

Tenet One

Research-Based Practice	Current Status	Priority Status	Data Sources and Collection Processes
1. We promote the health and well-being of each of our students.	4 3 2 1 0	4 3 2 1 0	
2. Our school upholds social justice and equity concepts.	4 3 2 1 0	4 3 2 1 0	
3. We provide a safe and supportive environment for each student.	4 3 2 1 0	4 3 2 1 0	
4. We encourage the active participation and empowerment of each student.	4 3 2 1 0	4 3 2 1 0	
5. Our school links health and education issues and systems.	4 3 2 1 0	4 3 2 1 0	
6. We address the health and well-being issues of each staff member.	4 3 2 1 0	4 3 2 1 0	
7. We collaborate with parents and the local community to promote the health and well-being of each student.	4 3 2 1 0	4 3 2 1 0	
8. We integrate health and well-being into the school's ongoing activities, curriculum, and assessment standards.	4 3 2 1 0	4 3 2 1 0	
9. We set realistic goals for student and staff health built on accurate data and sound science.	4 3 2 1 0	4 3 2 1 0	
10. We monitor the implementation of health and human services for the purpose of continuous improvement.	4 3 2 1 0	4 3 2 1 0	

Based on our initial analysis, we make the following recommendations:

1. The following are our initial priority areas for Tenet One:

2. We analyze data for the following priority areas:

3. We acquire or develop data sources and related analytical processes for the following areas:

4. We recommend that the following individuals and stakeholder groups be invited to help us in this process:

5. We suggest the following preliminary time line for this work:

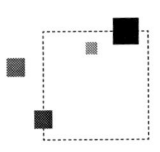

Action Tools Three–Seven: Planning and Implementing Professional Development for Tenet One

PURPOSE OF THESE TOOLS

This set of action tools will help your team design and implement professional development activities to support your Tenet One work.

HOW TO USE THE TOOLS

Determine which tools match the needs of the group with which you will be using them. Customize the professional development activities to align with the needs and goals of the group.

TIPS AND VARIATIONS

- ✓ Consult with your district wellness team, school health advisory council, or school health team to build on the work already under way.
- ✓ Determine if initial staff and stakeholder orientation sessions are necessary to ensure a common understanding and knowledge base about the links between health and learning to develop and implement a Tenet One–specific professional development program.
- ✓ Initiate study groups (using the resources included with this section) that include individuals with a high interest in this area.
- ✓ As study groups extend and refine their individual and collaborative knowledge and understanding, they can eventually evolve into problem-solving inquiry teams that merge into collaborative action research projects.
- ✓ Incorporate findings and recommendations from the collaborative inquiry group's work into a full-staff professional development plan and your school or district's strategic planning process.

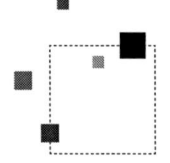

Action Tool Three: A Suggested Agenda for Your Tenet One Professional Development Activities

Objectives: Participants will be able to—

1. Describe the recommended practices associated with Tenet One of the Whole Child Compact: (a) creating healthy schools, (b) access to services that enable students to enter schools healthy, and (c) helping students learn about health and practice healthy decision making.
2. Examine their interactions with students and among themselves in relation to promoting Tenet One priorities.
3. Make recommendations for areas in which the school can improve to support Tenet One practices.

Suggested Professional Development Activities and Related Resources:

- Identifying Key Players in Your Tenet One Strategic Planning Process (The Players Chart—Who Are Your Players?)
- Each Student Learns About and Practices a Healthy Lifestyle—Creating Characteristics of a Healthy School (trio discussion)
- Helping Each Student Enter School Healthy and Ready to Learn (note-taking activity)
- Helping Adults Practice and Model Healthy Behaviors for Students (gallery walk)
- Final Remarks and Recommendations
- Suggested Action Steps: Planning Follow-Up for Potential Study Groups, Inquiry Teams, and Action Research Projects

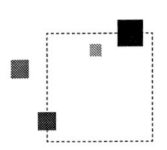

Action Tool Four: Identifying Key Players in Your Tenet One Strategic Planning Process

DIRECTIONS:

STEP 1:
For each of the 11 characteristics, list at least one person that you have involved or plan to involve in the assessment of that characteristic. You may list more than one person per category. One person may serve in multiple roles (i.e., as an expert, stakeholder, and champion).

Definitions:
Expert—A person with a high degree of skill in or knowledge of a certain subject
Stakeholder—A person who has a share or an interest, as in an enterprise
Consumer—A person who uses goods or services
Champion—An ardent defender or supporter of a cause

STEP 2:
Review the people listed and determine if you have missed anyone. If so, add their names to the chart.

STEP 3:
By each person's name, identify which people are Mavens (M), Connectors (C), or Salespeople (S).

Definitions:
Mavens—People who know a lot about a specific area of knowledge
Connectors—People who know and talk to a lot of different people
Salespeople—People who can sell anything to anyone

Identifying Key Players in Your Tenet One Strategic Planning Process

THE PLAYERS CHART—WHO ARE YOUR PLAYERS?

Directions: There are 11 structural factors (characteristics) in a school that need to be present to ensure a health-promoting school. These 11 characteristics are an expansion of the eight components of school health. Complete the chart to identify and communicate with team members and the public those involved in your Tenet One efforts.

Characteristic	Ideas and Recommendations for Next Steps:			
	Expert	**Stakeholder**	**Consumer**	**Champion**
1. Social and emotional school climate				
2. Family and community involvement				
3. School facilities and transportation quality				
4. Health education				
5. Physical education and physical activity				
6. Food and nutrition services				
7. School health services				
8. Counseling, psychological, and social services				
9. School-site health promotion for staff				
10. Coordination				
11. Policy and strategic planning				

Action Tool Five: Characteristics of a Healthy School

TRIO DISCUSSION

Directions:
Distribute the list of characteristics to each person.

Form trios. Assign each group three or four characteristics to discuss, ensuring that each characteristic is assigned to at least two groups.

Trio Discussion Questions:
How effectively do our school and district address the characteristics of a healthy school? In what areas would we recommend enhancement or improvement? What do we consider the most immediate priorities among our recommendations? What data do we need to collect?

The activity ends with each trio contributing to a group synthesis/summary of recommendations to be submitted to the larger whole group of training participants.

CHARACTERISTIC 1: School Health Program Policy and Strategic Planning: Our school maintains a culture that supports health through compliance with comprehensive policies that address all aspects of a coordinated approach to school health.

CHARACTERISTIC 2: Coordination of School Health Programs: The culture in our school facilitates coordination of all health programs to eliminate gaps and overlaps, expand access to health resources, and ensure high quality.

CHARACTERISTIC 3: Social and Emotional Climate: The culture in our school is conducive to making students, families, and members feel safe, secure, accepted, and valued.

CHARACTERISTIC 4: Family and Community Involvement: The culture in our school encourages, supports, and facilitates involvement of parents and guardians and the broader community in health programming.

CHARACTERISTIC 5: School Facilities and Transportation: The culture in our school ensures that buildings, grounds, and vehicles are secure and meet all established safety and environmental standards.

CHARACTERISTIC 6: Health Education: The culture in our school strongly supports and reinforces the health literacy knowledge, attitudes, behaviors, and skills students learn through a high-quality curriculum that meets health education standards.

CHARACTERISTIC 7: Physical Education and Physical Activity: The culture in our school strongly supports and reinforces the lifelong fitness knowledge, attitudes, behaviors, and skills students learn through a high-quality curriculum that meets physical education standards.

CHARACTERISTIC 8: Food and Nutrition Services: The culture in our school supports, promotes, and reinforces healthy eating patterns and food safety for students and staff.

CHARACTERISTIC 9: School Health Services: The culture in our school ensures student access to primary prevention, intervention, and treatment of disease and medical disorders.

CHARACTERISTIC 10: Counseling, Psychological, and Social Work Services: The culture in our school ensures student access to primary prevention, intervention, and treatment of mental health and substance abuse problems.

CHARACTERISTIC 11: School-Site Health Promotion for Staff: The culture in our school ensures high-level job performance and healthy role models for students by supporting and facilitating the physical and mental health and well-being of all employees.

Here is our trio's summary:

Characteristics discussed:

How effectively do our school and district address these characteristics of a healthy school?

In what areas would we recommend enhancement or improvement?

What do we consider the most immediate priorities among our recommendations?

What data do we need to collect?

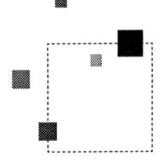

Action Tool Six: Helping Each Student Enter School Healthy and Ready to Learn

DIRECTIONS:

Divide participants into three groups.

Each group receives four statements.

Post the following guide:
- * We're there
- ! Let's go
- ? Not yet

Individually, participants read and rate the statement using the posted guide.

As a group, participants must agree on all *, !, or ?

Sheets representing the group's thinking with the appropriate marks are turned in. This information is used in planning.

Helping Each Student Enter School Healthy and Ready to Learn

1. Each student's needs (e.g., physical, mental, developmental) have been identified to ensure that the school program successfully addresses those needs).

2. Each student has appropriate background knowledge (e.g., alphabet, numbers) and social skills to enter the school prepared to learn.

3. Each student demonstrates appropriate attitudes about education and its purpose.

4. Each student uses knowledge and skills gained in health education and through experiences offered in school to make appropriate and healthy behavior choices.

5. Universal pre-school is available in the community to serve each child.

6. Local public health agencies work with schools to offer relevant and legally mandated vaccinations for each child.

7. Local public health and human services agencies work with schools to provide early identification services and support services for each child.

8. The school offers on-site or community health services for student immunizations and to address vision, hearing, dental, orthopedic, and mental health concerns for each child.

9. School outreach workers connect families to social services and health services through home visits to ensure the health and well-being of each child.

10. The school engages families in developing home support for education and its purposes so that every entering student is successful.

11. Parenting education programs are available in the community.

12. The school is linked with pre-school and child care programs to support the use of appropriate early child development curriculums.

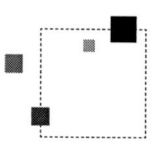

Action Tool Seven: Helping Adults Practice and Model Healthy Behaviors for Students

ACTIVITY—GALLERY WALK

Directions:
Post each question on a piece of chart paper.
Assign each question to a small group.
Give group members five minutes to chart responses to the question.
Instruct group members to place a check next to responses they deem to be most important.
After five minutes, rotate groups to the next chart.
After groups have visited all charts, distribute three dots to each participant.
Ask participants to place the dots next to the three responses they consider to be the most important.
Use this information to develop priority areas for the action plan.

HELPING ADULTS PRACTICE HEALTHY BEHAVIORS

Gallery Walk
1. To what extent do we have adequate opportunities to participate in on-site physical activity programs?
2. How does our school encourage us to participate in self-improvement activities on health-related topics?
3. To what extent does our school or district provide us with access to basic health screenings (e.g., health risk appraisal, blood pressure, blood lipids, height and weight)?
4. How are rewards used to motivate staff members' participation in health activities?
5. How do cross-institutional partnerships (e.g., with local hospitals, clinics, health organizations in the community) support our staff health initiatives?
6. To what extent are employee assistance programs in our district adequate to meet the needs of all staff members and their families?
7. How do we collaborate to identify and model behavior for each of our students to encourage them to understand and make wise decisions about health, safety, and behavior?
8. To what extent do our classrooms reflect our school vision, mission, and goals for healthy student behaviors and healthy staff behaviors?
9. What training and resources would be beneficial for addressing this Whole Child priority (i.e., helping adults model and practice healthy behaviors for students)?
10. How can we improve our outreach to parents and community members in helping us to address this priority?

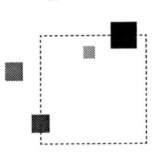

Action Tool Eight: Study Group Articles and Discussion Questions

PURPOSE OF THIS TOOL

This tool provides suggestions for *Educational Leadership* articles in electronic format for use in your Tenet One study groups. The electronic articles are available for download at www.ascd.org/downloads.

HOW TO USE THIS TOOL

Refer to the study guideline and tools included in the Overview section to support the planning and implementation of your study group.

Study Group Articles and Discussion Questions

1. **Susan B. Neuman. (2007, October). Changing the odds.** *Educational Leadership, 65*(2), 16–21.

   - What is early intervention? How can it be used to help students enter school healthy and be prepared for learning?
   - What does research tell us about helping economically disadvantaged students to enter school healthy and succeed academically?
   - How might we make use of the following strategies: targeting, developmental timing, intensity, professional training, coordinated services, compensatory instruction, and accountability?
   - Who do we need to collaborate with to improve the lives of our students?

2. **Ruby Payne (2008, April). Nine powerful practices.** *Educational Leadership, 65*(7), 48–52.

   - How can we collaborate to build relationships of respect within the school?
   - What are strategies for assessing each student's resources (e.g., financial, emotional, mental, spiritual, physical, support systems, relationships and role models, knowledge of unspoken rules)?
   - How can we teach students the "hidden rules of school"?
   - What can we do to monitor each student's progress and plan interventions?
   - How can we translate the concrete into the abstract for each student?
   - How can we teach students to ask questions?
   - How can we forge relationships with parents?

3. **David Satcher (2005, September). Healthy and ready to learn.** *Educational Leadership, 62*(1), 26–30.

   - In this article, Satcher summarizes a large body of research that shows how nutrition and physical activity affect student academic achievement. What are the major conclusions he presents?
   - Within your district, what are the current initiatives, resources, and programs that ensure students enter school healthy, based on the criteria identified by Satcher?
   - What are the implications of this article for your work with the Whole Child?
   - How might you reinforce and/or enhance cross-institutional collaboration to improve the health of entering students within your school or district?

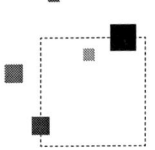

> # Action Tool Nine: Inquiry Team and Action Research Questions

PURPOSE OF THIS TOOL
This tool will support your planning process for the tenet and also guide implementation and evaluation of what is working.

HOW TO USE THIS TOOL
Determine which questions are aligned with your school community's needs and goals. Use the inquiry and action research tools included in the Overview section to guide your work.

TIPS AND VARIATIONS
✓ Have small groups select three to five different inquiry or action research questions as a focus area. Share plans and actions resulting from discussions and action research results in ongoing learning community meetings.

Inquiry Team and Action Research Questions

Tenet One Inquiry Focus Questions

1. How successfully do we coordinate school health services and program components? In what areas might we improve?
2. To what extent does each student in our school or district enter school healthy? How do we know?
3. What is a healthy school? To what extent does our school reflect the characteristics of a healthy organization?
4. How successfully does our school or district address extraordinary needs of individual students? What improvements are needed in such areas as interventions for individual learners' physical disabilities, mental impairment, social-relational issues, and psychological problems?
5. How do we know if each student has appropriate background knowledge and social skills to enter the school prepared to learn?
6. What attitudes does each student express about school, education, and the role of health, mental health, and positive behavior in promoting academic achievement? How do we know? How can we determine and address issues of concern?
7. How well do the school and community reinforce what students learn in health education?
8. How successful is our school or district at ensuring that our health education curriculum meets national curriculum standards?
9. How successful are we at promoting the health of every stakeholder in our learning community? How could we improve in the aggregate? How could we improve our work with specific individuals and subgroups?
10. To what extent does each student in our school make appropriate and healthy behavior choices? How can we identify problems or negative trends in this area for individual learners, subgroups, and whole groups of students?
11. How effectively does our school or district work with health agencies to support student physical and mental well-being? How can we expand our efforts in this area? How well do our efforts in this area meet national standards?
12. How efficient and productive are our current early identification services and programs? In what areas do they require improvement?
13. To what extent do families and students have ease of access to local public health and human service agencies? In what areas are improvements and modifications needed?
14. How effectively do our school outreach workers connect families and students to social and health services they need?
15. How effective are our school-based health advisory organizations, including our district wellness team and school health advisory council? How might they collaborate with community organizations to expand the availability of services?
16. To what extent do our school facilities and grounds support the learning process of each student? How might we make improvements in key areas we identify?
17. What is the quality of school food services and choices for students at our school? How do we encourage students to make the healthy choices?
18. To what extent does each student make healthy food choices and practice good nutritional behaviors? How do we know? Do our school fund-raisers include only nonfood items?
19. How can we expand our outreach and training for parents and families related to nutrition and food safety guidelines?
20. On the basis of national standards, what is the quality of our physical education programs and facilities? Are there areas in which they might be improved to meet the needs of each student?

21. To what extent do all physical education programs and overall physical activities in our school or district help each student to understand the value of lifetime physical fitness?
22. To what extent do classrooms in our school use physical activity to enhance student engagement and learning? What professional development services and programs might we offer to improve in this area?
23. How do staff members model and reinforce for each student lifetime healthy behaviors, attitudes, and lifestyles? How do we know? How can we determine gaps or areas of omission in this area?
24. What is the quality of our health education programs? To what extent can they be improved? How can we use national standards to guide our program evaluation process in this area?

Tenet One Action Research Questions
1. How can we help each student to enter school healthy? How will specific early interventions in this area contribute to the success of each student?
2. How can teacher modeling and coaching encourage each student to develop healthy attitudes about school and the importance of learning? What is the value added of emphasizing this component in our instructional program?
3. To what extent can we support individual students' extraordinary needs involving such areas as physical, mental, and social development?
4. What would be the impact of a specific early intervention (e.g., phonics program, vocabulary acquisition program) on the development of early learners' background knowledge in preparation for school entry?
5. How can our preK and kindergarten teachers work with parents, guardians, and families to improve the social skills of entering students?
6. To what extent does emphasizing certain knowledge and skills with each student improve his or her ability to make appropriate and healthy behavioral choices?
7. How do key aspects of pre-school programs influence students' ability to enter school healthy and ready to learn?
8. To what extent would the development and implementation of a pre-school parenting education program in our community support students' success as they enter school?
9. How will expanding our work with local public health agencies enhance our data on relevant and legally mandated vaccinations?
10. What effect will on-site health services have on student immunizations and such issues as vision, hearing, dental, orthopedic, and mental health?
11. How can we expand and improve the effectiveness of our wellness team and our school health team?
12. To what extent will expanding stakeholder participation on our wellness team or school health advisory council enhance its effectiveness?
13. How can we expand student and family access to social and health services offered by school outreach workers?
14. What is a health-promoting school according to international standards and models (e.g., the Coordinated School Health Approach advocated by the Centers for Disease Control and standards identified by the World Health Organization)? To what extent can we improve our school's profile using those criteria?
15. To what extent does our health education curriculum conform to National Health Education standards? How can we make substantive improvements in one or more identified areas?

16. What are research-proven strategies for eliminating or minimizing such issues as bullying and sexual harassment? To what extent will adoption schoolwide, by grade level, or by classroom of one or more of these strategies improve conditions related to these problems?
17. How can we develop and implement a process for monitoring school health conditions and practices (e.g., storage of toxic materials, safety of facilities and equipment, school crisis plans) and maximize their effectiveness?
18. How can we collaborate with food services staff to improve the food choices available for our students?
19. How can we collaborate with families and community stakeholders to ensure students' access to and choice of nutritious and safe foods?
20. To what extent do students engage in physical activity throughout their day? How can we expand the integration of physical activity and movement in all classrooms? What effect will this expansion have on academic achievement?
21. What are lifetime healthy behaviors? How can we improve our students' understanding of them?
22. How can staff collaborate on understanding and modeling healthy behaviors for students?
23. How can we enhance our assessment of students' knowledge and skills related to key facets of health education? How can we ensure that our health education programs and curricula are developmentally appropriate and engaging for each student?
24. How will expanding our cross-institutional partnerships involving health and mental health affect our students' academic performance?

TENET TWO TOOLS

Creating Intellectually Challenging Learning Environments That Are Physically and Emotionally Safe

INTRODUCTION 97

TITLE OF TOOL

1. Orientation, Group Discussion, and Initial Activities Exploring Key Criteria Associated with Tenet Two. 99

2. Examining Your School's Current Status—Suggested Strategies for Data Collection and Analysis for Tenet Two. 101

3. Examining Research-Based Best Practices for Tenet Two 103

4–7: Planning and Implementing Professional Development for Tenet Two. 109

    4. A Suggested Agenda for Your Tenet Two Professional Development Activities 110

    5. What Do We Know About Intellectually Challenging Learning Environments?. 111

    6. Identifying Curriculum, Assessment, and Instructional Practices That Promote Intellectual Challenge for Each Student. 113

    7. Ensuring That Each Student and Staff Member Feels Physically and Emotionally Safe 116

8. Study Group Articles and Discussion Questions 119

9. Inquiry Team and Action Research Questions 121

Creating Intellectually Challenging Learning Environments That Are Physically and Emotionally Safe

Introduction

This section will help educators and community members to address two primary goals: (1) to ensure that each student participates in intellectually challenging learning environments, and (2) to ensure that learning environments are physically and emotionally safe. These goals are inextricably tied to one another: An extensive body of contemporary educational research confirms that students cannot experience their education as intellectually challenging if they do not experience a sense of safety in their physical environment or if they lack a sense of emotional security in their classroom or school.

Intellectual challenge is a concept most often associated with the idea of rigor. Every student should be expected to master key curriculum standards that are challenging, exciting, and relevant. Such standards should reflect the best in what we know about the knowledge, skills, understanding, and habits of mind necessary for success in the 21st century global environment. Although we must hold every student accountable for the same rigorous and challenging standards, we must also make certain that learning conditions accommodate the individual readiness levels, interests, and learning profiles of every child.

As we shall see in this section, a challenging curriculum, assessment, and instructional program for every student requires an emphasis upon authenticity and real-world connections. Students should be able to see the purpose of their curriculum content and its relevance to themselves as individuals, to the community, and to the world they inhabit. A challenging, rigorous education also stresses such universal practices as inquiry-based learning, problem solving and decision making, experiential learning, and benchmark assessments that are performance and reality based.

Schools and communities committed to educating the whole child work together to ensure the physical and emotional safety and security of each child. They engage students in character education, peer mediation, conflict resolution, and similar programs to both ensure their safety in school and develop the skills, attitudes, and behaviors they will need to remain safe.

Every school has students who feel invisible, alienated, and alone. The extent to which schools and communities are willing to face that reality together determines the real safety of the learning environment. "With every interaction in a school, we are either building community or destroying it," says James Comer, founder of the School Development Program and Whole Child Commission member. In many cases the challenge of building whole communities necessitates difficult dialogue and a willingness to confront our deepest differences. As schools and communities commit to teaching young people the skills to think critically and engage in thoughtful debate, we adults must also have the courage to seek solutions rather than blame.

Like every section of this ASCD action tool, Section Two will provide you with a wide range of resources, suggestions, and action tool materials to help your Whole Child strategic planning team engage stakeholders in investigating these important issues. Once again, they are organized to parallel the other sections of this action tool, reinforcing the interrelationships and connections to be found in all of the Whole Child tenets.

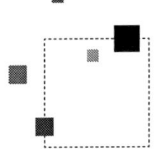

Action Tool One: Orientation, Group Discussion, and Initial Activities Exploring Key Criteria Associated with Tenet Two

PURPOSE OF THIS TOOL

Tenet Two in the Whole Child Compact emphasizes the need for every child to experience education as intellectually challenging. It also stresses that intellectual challenge and rigor are best manifested in learning environments that are both physically and emotionally safe for all participants (i.e., adults and students). This tool introduces the range of recommendations and processes advocated by the Whole Child Compact to achieve the goals of helping students to experience intellectual challenge and rigor within the context of a safe, orderly, and inviting learning environment.

HOW TO USE THIS TOOL

This tool offers a rich range of ideas and recommendations for your team's work with Tenet Two. It can also be used to facilitate staff discussions concerning key elements of Tenet Two. Whole Child strategic planning teams may elect to use this tool for stakeholder discussions, including analyzing gaps and omissions in classroom practices that weaken students' experience of intellectual rigor. It can also be used to investigate initial ideas for enhancing the school's levels of physical and emotional safety as part of building a positive and nurturing organizational climate. Perhaps most important, this tool can be used in a variety of venues to establish stakeholder consensus about the status of current Tenet Two instructional practices, services, and programs—and areas in which immediate and long-term work may need to occur.

TIPS AND VARIATIONS

- ✓ This tool can be used to support an initial study group involving members of your Whole Child strategic planning team. Use the materials and activities included here to focus members' understanding of the major structural components associated with successful Tenet Two implementation.
- ✓ This tool can also be used with stakeholder conversations and strategic planning sessions dedicated to identifying priorities related to such issues as curriculum mapping and revision, and enhanced emphasis upon rigor and excellence in your instructional and assessment systems.
- ✓ You can also use the ideas and strategies presented here as part of your work to improve student and adult perceptions of safety—both physical and emotional. These elements are powerfully aligned with the previous tenet because they are essential elements of a healthy learning organization that promotes healthy behaviors for all participants.

Orientation, Group Discussion, and Initial Activities Exploring Key Criteria Associated with Tenet Two

DIRECTIONS:

Write each question below on a sheet of chart paper and post the sheets around the room. Direct the participants to choose three to four questions that are of interest to them. Participants will visit each question for 5 to 10 minutes and discuss their thinking with other participants who have joined them. When time has expired, participants will move to the next question and begin another discussion with a new group of people. Information gained from this activity can be used to support future action planning focused on Tenet Two.

1. What does it mean for students to be intellectually challenged? What should we observe in classrooms when every student experiences intellectual challenge?
2. What are the behaviors and habits of mind students and staff demonstrate in classrooms in which intellectual challenge is the norm rather than the exception?
3. What kinds of instructional strategies and techniques would you expect in classrooms with teachers who intellectually challenge each of their students?
4. What does it mean to feel physically safe in a school building or classroom?
5. What conditions and practices ensure that a building or classroom is physically safe for every student?
6. What does it mean to feel emotionally safe in a school building or classroom?
7. What conditions and practices ensure that a building or classroom is emotionally safe for every student?
8. How would you summarize the characteristics of our building and the classrooms in it? To what extent do you believe that all our classrooms are intellectually challenging, physically safe, and emotionally safe?

What are our conclusions and recommendations in these areas of Tenet Two?

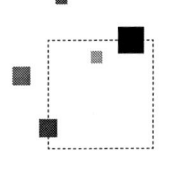

Action Tool Two: Examining Your School's Current Status—Suggested Strategies for Data Collection and Analysis for Tenet Two

PURPOSE OF THIS TOOL

As your Whole Child strategic planning team completes its preliminary discussion and analysis of Tenet Two programs and practices in your school or district, a logical next step will be preliminary data collection and analysis related to your recommendations. This tool will provide a process and methodology for your team to begin determining how accurate your initial insights and recommendations were, based on available student, staff, and related stakeholder data involving intellectual rigor in all classrooms, student and staff perceptions of physical safety within the building, and student and staff perceptions of emotional safety within the context of school climate.

HOW TO USE THIS TOOL

Examine the recommendations presented here in this tool. Then, consider the available evidence (e.g., formal student and program evaluation data) to determine the extent to which each element or strategy is fully operational. For areas in which there may be insufficient data to allow valid conclusions, consider how your team might acquire those data to make valid inferences and recommendations for program development and school change in relationship to key Tenet Two focus areas.

TIPS AND VARIATIONS

✓ Use this tool and the analytical processes it generates to determine key elements of your Tenet Two work. For example, Who should be the key players in bringing about change and transformation? Who needs to be involved to address Tenet Two gaps and emerging priorities and goals? How should we involve the community? How will students be involved in making change occur, including potential service learning projects?

✓ Once again, be certain to communicate your conclusions and recommendations to members of your school improvement team(s) as well as other relevant stakeholders and stakeholder groups. A key goal should be the alignment of all Whole Child work with the learning organization's commitment to holistic, unified, and coherent educational transformation. Tenet Two's focus on intellectual rigor, for example, is closely aligned with Tenet Three's ideas about the importance of student engagement in promoting high levels of achievement for all.

✓ At the completion of the discussion and analysis process facilitated through Action Tool Two, it will be an ideal time for your Whole Child strategic planning team to engage in outreach to individuals and organizations that can support your recommended changes. In addition to finding experts (e.g., university researchers, program directors, central office leaders) who can help you with your work, you will need to start the conversation: How will we fund and sustain recommended organizational changes? Will our expanded emphasis on intellectual rigor necessitate additional resources such as time for professional development? How can cross-institutional partnerships (e.g., with local universities) support us in achieving our vision for renewal in key Tenet Two areas?

Action Tool Two: Examining Your School's Current Status—
Suggested Strategies for Data Collection and Analysis for Tenet Two

Examining Your School's Current Status—Suggested Strategies for Data Collection and Analysis for Tenet Two

Suggested Discussion Questions for Data Collection and Analysis	Questions and Recommendations	Recommended Resources
How do we communicate and maintain behavioral expectations, rules, and routines for everyone in our learning community?		
How do these expectations, rules, and routines contribute to our school's organizational climate?		
How do we make certain that expectations, rules, and routines are administered equitably to promote the success of each student?		
To what extent do we have early-intervention systems in place to identify and lessen the impact of potential behavior issues and disciplinary problems?		
How do we welcome families and community members into our school? What do we communicate through this process?		
How effective are our extracurricular activities in providing challenge and relevance for every student?		
To what extent is every classroom in our school intellectually challenging? What criteria do we use to determine intellectual challenge?		
To what extent does every student experience intellectual challenge in every classroom? How can we tell?		
How do our teachers employ active and experiential learning strategies (e.g., experiential learning, inquiry-based learning, authentic culminating projects) to challenge every student?		
Overall, how safe is our building? To what extent does each participant feel physically and emotionally safe here? How do we know?		

Initial Reflections and Recommendations for Tenet Two:

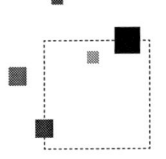

Action Tool Three: Examining Research-Based Best Practices for Tenet Two

PURPOSE OF THIS TOOL

Tenet Two presents an interesting challenge for Whole Child strategic planning teams because, on its surface, it seems to juxtapose two seemingly disconnected areas of emphasis: that is, intellectual challenge and building safety. This tool will provide a synthesis of the research literature that confirms the close alignment between these two factors. In particular, the research seems to confirm that without students, faculty, and staff experiencing a sense of physical safety and emotional support with the school climate, maximizing intellectual rigor and challenge for many students becomes difficult, if not impossible.

HOW TO USE THIS TOOL

This tool can be used as part of your strategic planning process for Tenet Two. It can also be used with a variety of stakeholder groups interested in developing a basic knowledge and understanding of the implications of Tenet Two for school reform and transformation. You may also elect to use this tool with parent, community, and related stakeholder constituencies to bring about consensus about where you are heading and why you are going there with various components of Tenet Two. An essential question for this tenet involves student, family, and community feedback on levels of challenge and rigor for every student—both within the formal curriculum and in extracurricular activities available to every student.

TIPS AND VARIATIONS

- ✓ Continue to emphasize the alignment and interrelationships among the various Whole Child Tenets. For example, how do your results from using this action tool align with your commitments to helping each student experience the learning environment as engaging and sensitive to personal interests and needs?
- ✓ Use the ideas and strategies presented here as a springboard for potential cross-institutional partnership work with such agencies as universities within your community. They can be very powerful allies in helping educators keep up-to-date about the latest developments in a content area or academic field. Cross-institutional partnerships in this area are especially important when you are considering changes in the physical plant, technology upgrades, enhancement of school culture, and related resource acquisition to address safety issues.
- ✓ Make certain that you share your conclusions and recommendations with your school improvement or district strategic planning team(s) to reinforce effective collaboration and a seamless, holistic approach to school reform and transformation. This tenet clearly requires sensitivity to work within and across planning teams dealing with health, behavior, and safe decision making among students and staff members.

Examining Research-Based Best Practices for Tenet Two

This matrix can be used in a variety of ways, including (1) as a classroom observation walk-through tool, (2) to initiate community conversations related to this particular tenet, (3) to promote staff discussions of how successfully a school is preparing each student for college and postgraduation study, (4) to facilitate stakeholder discussions of the extent to which a school is successfully preparing each student for work in a global environment, and (5) as initial strategic planning for professional development as part of your school improvement planning process.

As you consider the skills, competencies, and recommended practices, rate your school or district on the extent to which each plays a key part in each student's education:

4 = High degree of evidence; 3 = Adequate degree of evidence; 2 = Some degree of evidence, but needs further attention; 1 = Minimum degree of evidence with the need for much more attention; 0 = No evidence with major need for attention and emphasis.

Part I: Student Competencies	Rating
When students are successful in intellectually challenging learning environments that are both physically and emotionally safe, research confirms that they exhibit the following behaviors:	
1. Each student exercises motor control reflecting executive brain functions (e.g., restraining impulsivity).	4 3 2 1 0
2. Each student demonstrates viable and effective decision-making skills, avoiding risky or health-threatening behaviors.	4 3 2 1 0
3. Each student demonstrates a sense of personal efficacy and prosocial behaviors.	4 3 2 1 0
4. Each student displays a capacity for self-regulation and self-monitoring reflective of mental health.	4 3 2 1 0
5. Each student seeks help when necessary to resolve problems and exercise prosocial behavior.	4 3 2 1 0
Recommendations and Conclusions for Part I	

Action Tool Three: Examining Research-Based Best Practices for Tenet Two

Tenet Two Research-Based Organizational Practices (School Level)	Rating
1. Each student learns in an intellectually challenging environment that is physically and emotionally safe for students and adults—that is, each student feels physically safe and demonstrates prosocial behavior (i.e., respect for the physical safety of others).	4 3 2 1 0
2. School buildings, grounds, and vehicles are secure and meet all established safety and environmental standards.	4 3 2 1 0
3. The school physical plant is attractive, structurally sound, has good internal (hallways) and external (pedestrian and motor vehicle) traffic flow, and is free of defects.	4 3 2 1 0
4. School staff, students, and family members establish and maintain classroom behavioral expectations, rules, and routines:	
• The clarity, appropriateness, and equitable implementation of behavioral expectations, rules, and procedures contribute to the school's climate and organization.	4 3 2 1 0
• Students, staff, and family members perceive the school as a learning community that is safe, orderly, and inviting for all.	4 3 2 1 0
• The school has clearly articulated rules and procedures that are communicated and implemented consistently and equitably.	4 3 2 1 0
• Classroom rules and procedures are clearly articulated and consistently implemented for all students.	4 3 2 1 0
• Parents and guardians are actively involved in reinforcing behavioral expectations, rules, and routines.	4 3 2 1 0
• Parents, guardians, and community members are provided regular opportunities for training and support in reinforcing the school's expectations, rules, and routines.	4 3 2 1 0
• School staff and parents model sustained prosocial behaviors.	4 3 2 1 0
• The school maintains a clearly articulated process for addressing student infractions of rules and procedures.	4 3 2 1 0
• Early intervention systems are in place to ensure that potentially disruptive situations and disciplinary infractions are minimized.	4 3 2 1 0
5. Families are welcomed by school staff as partners in their children's education:	
• Structures and methods are in place to ensure that all family members can communicate directly with the school and relevant staff members.	4 3 2 1 0
• The school staff employs a range of structures and methods to communicate to families and community members, ensuring that all stakeholders understand the school's vision, mission, goals, and expectations for learners.	4 3 2 1 0
• Family members and community members play an active role in school governance and management.	4 3 2 1 0

© 2008. All Rights Reserved.

Tenet Two Research-Based Organizational Practices (School Level) (continued)	Rating
6. The school provides access to rigorous programs in all content areas, including the arts, foreign language, and social studies:	
• All learners are required to investigate and understand the visual and performing arts as part of their core curriculum.	4 3 2 1 0
• Students receive appropriate opportunities to study and become fluent in one or more world languages.	4 3 2 1 0
• All learners are encouraged to understand the significance of language and linguistics as part of their development of communication proficiencies.	4 3 2 1 0
• Students are supported in understanding the nature of the globally interdependent workplace and the competencies necessary for success in the world of work today.	4 3 2 1 0
• Social studies courses and programs emphasize ethical citizenship and encourage students to understand their responsibilities as citizens of their own nation and as part of a globally interdependent community.	4 3 2 1 0
• As a result of their participation in social studies curricula and programs, students develop an understanding of diversity in the world today, including such focus areas as gender, race, ethnicity, religion, region, socioeconomic status, and culture.	4 3 2 1 0
• Classrooms emphasize higher-order reasoning reinforced through higher-order questioning as an instructional strategy.	4 3 2 1 0
• The curriculum emphasizes rigorous core standards that encourage every student to understand what he or she is learning and ways to apply it to the world beyond the classroom.	4 3 2 1 0
• Assessment practices are balanced and emphasize authentic assessments such as real-world culminating projects.	4 3 2 1 0
• Instructors encourage students to see the relevance in what they are doing and why they are doing it.	4 3 2 1 0
Our School District	
• Conducts regular school climate surveys of students, staff, and parents	4 3 2 1 0
• Develops school-based programs that involve students and staff, such as peer mediation and conflict resolution, to ensure a positive school climate	4 3 2 1 0
• Develops district policy for incorporating social and emotional development into the district's educational program	4 3 2 1 0

Tenet Two Research-Based Organizational Practices (School Level) (continued)	Rating
Our Community	
• Collaborates with school districts to provide learning opportunities such as apprenticeships and internships outside the classroom	4 3 2 1 0
• Collaborates with districts to support opportunities for student employment and involvement in community-based activities	4 3 2 1 0
• Collaborates to ensure young people have a variety of safe options for recreational and cultural activities outside school	4 3 2 1 0
Recommendations and Conclusions for Part II	

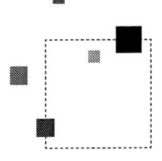

Action Tools Four–Seven: Planning and Implementing Professional Development for Tenet Two

PURPOSE OF THESE TOOLS

This set of action tools will help your team design and implement professional development activities to support your Tenet Two work.

HOW TO USE THE TOOLS

Determine which tools match the needs of the group you will be using them with. Customize the professional development activities aligned with the needs and goals of the group.

Included with these Tenet Two professional development action tools are the following resources and materials:

1. A Suggested Agenda for Your Tenet Two Professional Development Activities
2. What Do We Know About Intellectually Challenging Learning Environments?
3. Identifying Curriculum, Assessment, and Instructional Practices That Promote Intellectual Challenge for Each Student
4. Ensuring That Each Student and Staff Member Feels Physically and Emotionally Safe

TIPS AND VARIATIONS

- ✓ Determine if you wish to develop and implement a Tenet Two–specific professional development program involving initial staff orientation sessions to ensure a common understanding and knowledge base.
- ✓ If you have determined that intellectual challenge is to become a Whole Child priority for your school or district, you may wish to use all of the materials included here to develop and implement a complete orientation program for your staff and other stakeholder groups. Similarly, if physical and emotional safety appear to be a priority, you can use the resources included in this tool for that component.
- ✓ If your data analysis process suggests that only some aspects of Tenet Two are underemphasized or display gaps in performance, you may elect to use only those resources and suggestions that directly apply to your most immediate Tenet Two priorities.
- ✓ Subsequent to initial outreach trainings, you may decide to invite those participants with a high level of interest and expertise in Tenet Two areas to begin study groups (using the resources included with this section).
- ✓ As study groups extend and refine their individual and collaborative knowledge and understanding, their work can eventually evolve into problem-solving inquiry teams that emerge into collaborative action research projects involving promotion of intellectual rigor and physical and emotional safety.
- ✓ Ideally, the outcome of this job-embedded and collaborative inquiry work will be the incorporation of findings and recommended Tenet Two strategies into full-staff trainings and your school or district's strategic planning process for school reform and transformation.

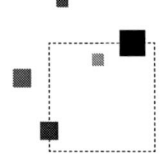

Action Tool Four: A Suggested Agenda for Your Tenet Two Professional Development Activities

Objectives: Participants will be able to—

- Explore and understand the key principles and recommended practices associated with Tenet Two of the Whole Child Compact: (1) intellectually challenging learning environments, (2) buildings and classrooms that are physically safe, and (3) buildings and classrooms that are emotionally safe
- Examine their own work with students and themselves in relationship to promoting Tenet Two priorities
- Make recommendations for areas in which they and the school might improve in identified Tenet Two priorities

SUGGESTED PROFESSIONAL DEVELOPMENT ACTIVITIES AND RELATED RESOURCES

- What Do We Know About Intellectually Challenging Learning Environments?
- Identifying Curriculum, Assessment, and Instructional Practices That Promote Intellectual Challenge for Each Student
- Ensuring That Each Student and Staff Member Feels Physically and Emotionally Safe
- Next Steps and Recommendations Based upon Our Activities Today
- Action Planning for Study Groups, Inquiry Teams, and Action Research Projects
- Concluding Discussion: How Does Tenet Two Apply to Our Current School Improvement Planning Process? How Can We Address Identified Tenet Two Priority Areas, Gaps, and Omissions via Collaborative Inquiry Processes?

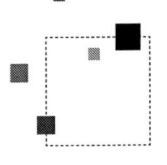

Action Tool Five: What Do We Know About Intellectually Challenging Learning Environments? A Professional Development Scavenger Hunt!

SUMMARY

This initial professional development activity is a variation on the scavenger hunt game. Participants are asked to team up with a partner. They are then asked to move around the school and identify at least one classroom or hallway artifact reflective of each of the characteristics of intellectual challenge presented below. A variation of this scavenger hunt would involve participants who are engaged in training during the school day. Their artifact collection might include observations of staff and student behavior reflective of intellectual engagement as well. (NOTE: Although not necessary, it would be a wonderful addition to this activity if participant teams each had a digital camera to photograph each artifact.)

DIRECTIONS:

- Today you will be participating in an old-fashioned scavenger hunt focusing on finding artifacts in our school that represent different aspects of intellectual challenge for our students.
- Form a partner team (two to three participants). As a team, review and discuss the artifact list presented below. This list showcases the categories of intellectual challenge that you will be searching for on your hunt.
- When you have collected examples of each artifact on your list, return to the training room. If other teams have also returned, use that time to share your collection and compare your impressions of the level of intellectual challenge evident in our school.
- At the conclusion of our scavenger hunt, we will share our collective impressions and formulate recommendations about areas in which we would like to see improvement or enhancement.

YOUR ARTIFACT CHALLENGE!

1. Find an example of a student work product that reflects a high level of commitment and dedication on the part of the learner.
2. Find a bulletin board display that acknowledges the range and complexity of student work products.
3. Find evidence of culminating performance tasks that are connected in some way to the world beyond the classroom.
4. Find an example of a culminating project that represents authentic, professional behaviors on the part of the learner, that is, he or she completed a complex task that has parallels in the professional context of the discipline studied (e.g., the work actually done by an artist, historian, scientist, mathematician, writer).
5. Find evidence that student work products are highly aligned with rigorous academic standards.
6. Find an example to confirm that the classroom does not emphasize worksheet activities but rather work products that require higher-order reasoning on the part of every student.
7. Find examples of questioning activities and strategies used by a teacher to confirm an emphasis on higher-order levels of questioning rather than on factual-recall questioning.
8. Find an example of technology being used to reinforce student information processing, collection, and analysis.
9. Find an example of technology-based simulations being used to complement students' investigation of an issue, theme, or idea.
10. Identify one or more ways in which an instructor organizes his or her curriculum conceptually around big ideas or essential questions.
11. Find evidence of how room arrangements reinforce intellectual challenge that is differentiated (rather than exclusive emphasis upon whole-group instruction).

Other examples you can find and share:

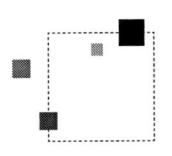

Action Tool Six: Identifying Curriculum, Assessment, and Instructional Practices That Promote Intellectual Challenge for Each Student—A Professional Development Grab Bag Activity

SUMMARY

Each participant "grabs" a card from the bag. On each card is the description of a curriculum, assessment, or instructional practice proven to promote intellectual challenge. In the time provided, participants should pair up with as many other individuals as possible to share their strategies. At the conclusion of the one-on-one section of the activity, participants return to their seats and write down as many strategies as they can remember. The activity concludes with individuals forming triads with two other participants to share their lists and their impressions of how many of the strategies and practices they perceive as actively in place in their classroom and school.

DIRECTIONS:

- You will be participating in a grab bag activity for this part of our training involving curriculum, instruction, and assessment strategies proven effective in promoting students' sense of intellectual challenge. Select one card from the bag. You will be responsible for understanding and explaining that strategy to other members of your training group.
- As you circulate to trade strategies, try to take no more than two to three minutes with each partner.
- Your facilitator will post time markers periodically to let you know how much time is left in the grab bag process.
- When time is called, please return to your seat and list as many of the strategies as you can recall.
- Then, form a triad with two other participants, comparing your lists. Close your discussion with reflections on how frequently these strategies appear to be used in classrooms within your school.
- If time permits, your facilitator will lead a discussion with the entire group, listing recommendations for specific action steps and priority areas involving the strategies you explored today.

GRAB BAG CARDS:

Curriculum, instruction, and assessment strategies that promote students' sense of intellectual challenge

---

HIGHER-ORDER QUESTIONING

Avoid emphasizing factual-recall questioning. At least 75 percent of your time, ask students higher-order questions that require them to analyze, synthesize, and evaluate key information, ideas, and themes.

WAIT TIME I AND II

Maximize the number of students who hear and decode your questions by waiting at least two to three seconds before eliciting a response (Wait Time I) and at least two to three seconds before giving the responding student a reaction (Wait Time II).

COMPARISON, CONTRAST, AND CLASSIFICATION

Ask students to find similarities, differences, and ways to categorize topics they have been studying. Encourage students to deep process information and ideas by creating original metaphors, similes, and analogies to express their insights about interrelationships.

CONCEPTUALLY ORGANIZING YOUR CURRICULUM

Help your students to see the "big picture" in your curriculum, especially how major ideas and themes interconnect and interrelate to form a unified whole. Use strategies such as essential questions, which ask students to investigate the big ideas of your curriculum via open-ended inquiry.

USE A BALANCED, AUTHENTIC APPROACH TO ASSESSMENT

Avoid depending exclusively on tests and quizzes for your assessment process. Balance them with more authentic forms of assessments, including student completion of academic prompts and projects that allow for authentic, real-world applications of what they have been learning.

ENGAGE STUDENTS IN SELF-ASSESSMENT AND METACOGNITION ACTIVITIES

Make certain that every student understands the evaluation criteria for which he or she is responsible. Encourage students to self-monitor using those criteria (especially via rubrics and scoring keys). In their academic notebooks, have students chart and reflect upon their progress in relationship to each learning goal and its related criteria.

USE HOOK ACTIVITIES AS WARM-UPS

Start your classes each day with some form of anticipatory set activity that challenges students and engages their imaginations. Use these short hook activities to encourage students to see what they are learning as significant and challenging—but fun.

MAKE A RANGE OF HIGH-INTEREST MATERIALS AVAILABLE TO EVERY STUDENT

Make an effort to have classroom resources and materials (including online, electronic resources) available so that students' individual interests and learning profiles can be accommodated. Whenever feasible, allow students to select the reading materials they will use to complete an assignment.

ALLOW STUDENTS TO COMPLETE ORBITAL PROJECTS

Think of your core curriculum as the sun in a solar system. Have every student master that core curriculum content and related standards, but periodically allow students to become "planets," encouraging them to investigate and report back on areas of content that interest them. For example, a student interested in music might research the music of an era being studied in a world history class.

USE PAIDEIA SEMINARS

Periodically have students break into small seminar groups. Have them appoint a facilitator, a recorder, a timekeeper, and a peacekeeper. Pose an interpretive question (or set of questions) students will discuss as they respond to a short text (print, electronic, visual or performing arts). At the conclusion of the seminar period, have students share their insights.

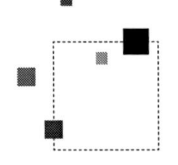

Action Tool Seven: Ensuring That Each Student and Staff Member Feels Physically and Emotionally Safe—A Paideia Seminar

> **SUMMARY**
>
> In this activity, participants will be asked to engage in a Paideia seminar focusing on ideas for promoting a physically and emotionally safe learning environment. Groups assemble in teams of four to five. They appoint an internal facilitator who manages the flow of the discussion, using the suggested interpretive questions below. Ideally, a recorder keeps track of ideas presented—and areas in which there is consensus or a lack of it. At the conclusion of this activity, teams reassemble as a whole group to discuss their insights, conclusions, and recommendations.

DIRECTIONS:

1. During this activity, you will be participating in a Paideia seminar focusing upon a reading selection that addresses the issue of making schools physically and emotionally safe for all participants.
2. To get started, form teams of four to five members. Assemble around a table so that you are facing one another.
3. Appoint a group facilitator (who will keep the conversation moving using the interpretive questions provided). Also, ask someone in your group to record the major ideas generated by participants, including highlighting areas of consensus and disagreement. Appoint a timekeeper who can also serve as a peacekeeper if conflicts emerge.
4. Periodically, your timekeeper should remind you of the time remaining. Your recorder should summarize what he or she considers key ideas and points of agreement and disagreement.
5. At the conclusion of the seminar, each team member should be asked to summarize their reactions, highlighting insights and questions raised by the experience.
6. If time permits, the various seminar teams should reassemble as a whole group to share their conclusions and recommendations based upon their interpretation of the reading selection.

PROVIDING A SAFE AND SECURE ENVIRONMENT FOR LEARNING: YOUR PAIDEIA SEMINAR READING SELECTION

Seminar Questions to Guide Your Discussion

1. According to this selection, what are the major characteristics of a school environment that is physically and emotionally safe for all participants?
2. What does each of the studies cited recommend about promoting physical and emotional safety in schools?
3. What are the commonalities shared by each of these studies?
4. What are your reactions to each of the recommendations presented here?
5. To what extent do the ideas in this reading selection have relevance to us as we work with Tenet Two's emphasis upon safe and orderly learning environments?

The ASCD publication *Creating a Healthy School Using the Healthy School Report Card* emphasizes that the social and emotional climate of a school should be conducive to making students, families, and staff members feel safe, secure, and accepted. For example, a student code of conduct and discipline clearly delineates behaviors that lead to suspension, expulsion, or other sanctions. School rules apply equally to students and staff. In addition, teachers must provide a robust curriculum based on their thorough knowledge of the subject and the methods most effective for teaching it. Essential content should be identified and each student has an opportunity to learn.

Similarly, the research publication entitled *Every Child Learning: Safe and Supportive Schools* (pp. 2–3) answers the following essential question: Why is a safe and supportive learning community so powerful? According to this report, such an environment fulfills students' basic psychological needs for belonging, autonomy, influence, competence, and physical security. As those basic needs are met, students tend to become increasingly committed to the school community's norms, rules, and values. As students subscribe more deeply to those constructive norms, their behavior changes accordingly, which in turn creates an upward spiral that benefits everyone.

The Health Behavior in School-Aged Children (HBSC) is a collaborative, cross-national study conducted on a four-year cycle that compares students around the world to "gain insight into, and increase understanding of, adolescent health behaviors, health, and lifestyles in their social context" (U.S. Department of Health and Human Services, 2003, p. 12). Among its most recent findings:

- Overall, U.S. youth are no more likely to be involved in bullying others at school than students in many other European countries and Canada.
- However, the United States is among the higher ranking countries for frequent bullying by students.
- Only 38 percent of U.S. students always feel safe at school, and 30 percent rarely or never feel safe.
- U.S. students are among the least likely to believe that their classmates are kind and helpful (only 39 percent of girls and 35 percent of boys), followed only by Lithuania and the Czech Republic. By comparison, 89 percent of girls and 90 percent of boys in Portugal, 65 percent of girls and 61 percent of boys in Israel, and 51 percent of girls and 44 percent of boys in Canada agree that their classmates are kind and helpful.

Such research has led to the development of many character education and school discipline programs. Research on programs emphasizing schoolwide conflict resolution, peer mediation, and direct teaching of social skills and self-management strategies has shown positive effects (Learning First Alliance, 2001).

Each learner deserves to be intellectually challenged by his or her educational experiences. At the same time, learning environments that address the needs of the whole child must be both physically and emotionally safe. In effect, they must be safe, orderly, and inviting communities of learning.

Students are most motivated to learn, feel the greatest sense of accomplishment, and achieve at the highest levels when they are able to succeed at tasks that spark their interest and stretch their capacities. To be meaningful, learning must effectively connect to students' questions, concerns, and personal experiences, thereby capturing their intrinsic motivation and making the value of what they learn readily apparent to them (Learning First Alliance, (2001).

There are numerous research-based climate survey reports associated with this tenet and its essential principles. For example, Where We Teach: The CUBE Survey of Urban School Climate (B.K. Perkins, NSBA, 2007), the second school climate survey conducted by the National School Boards Association's Council of Urban Boards of Education, reflects feedback from 12 participating districts and 4,700 teachers in 127 schools. According to this NSBA report (p. 6), the school climate—the impressions, beliefs, and expectations about a school as a learning environment—plays a critical role in the academic development of the student learner, and the administrators and teachers clearly and strongly influence that impression.

Finally, consider these recommendations for promoting a learning environment that is physically and emotionally safe for all participants:

1. Conduct regular school climate surveys of students, staff, and parents.
2. Develop school-based programs that involve students and staff, such as peer mediation and conflict resolution, to ensure a positive school climate.
3. Develop district policy for incorporating social and emotional development into the district's educational program.
4. Schools and communities committed to educating the whole child work together to ensure the physical and emotional safety and security of each child.
5. They consistently assess comprehensive safety issues to foster effective conditions for learning.

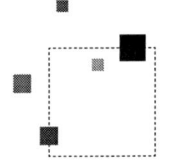

Action Tool Eight: Study Group Articles and Discussion Questions

PURPOSE OF THIS TOOL

This tool provides suggestions for *Educational Leadership* articles in electronic format for use in your Tenet Two study groups. The electronic articles are available for download at www.ascd.org/downloads.

HOW TO USE THIS TOOL

Refer to the study guideline and tools included in the Overview section to support the planning and implementation of your study group.

Study Group Articles and Discussion Questions

Promoting Intellectual Challenge for Each Student

1. **Thomas Armstrong (2007, May). The Curriculum Superhighway.** *Educational Leadership, 64*(8), 16–20.

   - What are the major problems in curriculum that Armstrong identifies in contemporary schools? To what extent does the curriculum of your district reflect these problems?
   - How might schools in your district work together to address the issues Armstrong identifies at the heart of "the Curriculum Superhighway"?
   - In the article, Armstrong makes recommendations about how students at various age levels require specific curriculum elements to ensure that they are intellectually challenged. What are the differences—and unifying components—that make for an intellectually challenging curriculum for each student?

2. **Arthur L. Costa (2008, February). The thought-filled curriculum.** *Educational Leadership, 65*(5), 20–24.

   - According to Costa, what is a "thought-filled curriculum"? To what extent do we have one in our school or district?
   - How successfully are we currently addressing Costa's five themes for a challenging curriculum for each student (learning to think, thinking to learn, thinking together, thinking about our own thinking, thinking big)?

3. **Carol Corbett Burns, Kevin G. Welner, Edward W. Wiley, & John Murphy (2007, April). A world-class curriculum for all.** *Educational Leadership, 64*(7), 53–56.

   - How do the authors recommend that schools address the parallel issues of equity and excellence?
   - What are the major design components of the International Baccalaureate program, as presented by the authors? How do these components support the goal of intellectually challenging each student?
   - What can you infer from this article about ways in which curriculum can address the needs of each learner while promoting success for all?

4. **Johanna Mustacchi (2008, March). What's relevant for YouTubers?** *Educational Leadership, 65*(6), 67–70.

   - What are Mustacchi's recommendations for making learning relevant to modern students?
   - According to Mustacchi, how does student exposure to media influence their concepts of intellectual challenge and the learning process?
   - What can we make of the case for media literacy presented by the author? What are its implications for our work in promoting intellectual challenge for each student?
   - How can we speak to what Mustacchi calls "the next generation"? To what extent are her recommendations relevant to our Whole Child Initiative?

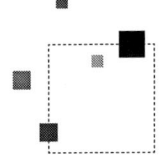

Action Tool Nine: Inquiry Team and Action Research Questions

PURPOSE OF THIS TOOL

This tool will support your planning process for the tenet and also guide implementation and evaluation of what is working.

HOW TO USE THIS TOOL

Determine which questions are aligned with your school community's needs and goals. Use the inquiry and action research tools included in the Overview section to guide your work.

TIPS AND VARIATIONS

✓ Have small groups select three to five different inquiry or action research questions as a focus area. Share plans and actions resulting from discussions, and action research results in ongoing learning community meetings.

Inquiry Team and Action Research Questions

Tenet Two Inquiry Focus Questions

1. To what extent does every student exercise motor control reflecting executive brain functions (e.g., restraining impulsivity)? How can we identify and address problems involving this brain-based issue?
2. How well do our students demonstrate viable and effective decision-making skills?
3. To what extent does each student avoid—or fail to avoid—risky or health-threatening behaviors? What are the consequences of a failure in this area?
4. To what extent does each student demonstrate a sense of personal efficacy? What are the effects of individual students' failure to perceive themselves as viable, contributing human beings?
5. How effectively do our students demonstrate prosocial behaviors? What are the causes of antisocial behavior and behavior patterns in individuals, subgroups, and whole groups of students?
6. How competent are our students in demonstrating the ability to self-regulate?
7. How is an individual student's failure to self-regulate and self-monitor reflective of problems in his or her mental health?
8. To what extent do our students seek help when necessary to resolve problems?
9. How effective—or ineffective—are our students' individual and collective approaches to problem solving?
10. To what extent does each student demonstrate pro-social behavior?
11. What are the consequences of students failing to exercise prosocial behavior?
12. How intellectually challenging is each classroom in our school? How do we know?
13. What are the consequences of boredom and lethargy for individual students? For classes of students?
14. To what extent do we contribute to each student's sense of intellectual challenge—or lack of intellectual challenge?
15. How effectively does our school provide access for every student to rigorous programs in all content areas, including the arts, foreign language, and social studies?
16. To what extent have we achieved consensus about what constitutes intellectual rigor in our classrooms and school?
17. To what extent are classrooms in our school physically safe for every student and staff member? How do we know?
18. To what extent are classrooms in our school emotionally safe for every student and staff member? How do we know?
19. How effectively does each of our students demonstrate prosocial behavior, expressing respect for the physical safety of others?
20. How efficient and effective are we in identifying and eliminating physical threats, incipient violence, and bullying?
21. To what extent are our school buildings, grounds, and vehicles secure? To what extent do they meet all established safety and environmental standards?
22. To what extent is our school's physical plant attractive and structurally sound, with good internal (hallways) and external (pedestrian and motor vehicle) traffic flow?
23. How efficient are we in identifying and addressing defects in internal and external physical plant structures, resources, and processes?
24. To what extent are all school staff, students, and family members in consensus about behavioral expectations, rules, and routines? What problems result when there is inconsistency in this area?
25. To what extent do families feel welcomed by school staff as partners in their children's education? How do we know?

26. To what extent have we implemented successful schoolwide programs and practices to promote social and emotional learning? How effectively have we determined the value they add to each student's well-being?
27. What evidence do we have—or lack—regarding the effect of schoolwide social and emotional learning programs and practices, including evidence-based sequenced instruction?

Tenet Two Suggested Action Research Questions
1. How can we help every student to exercise motor control reflecting executive brain functions (e.g., restraining impulsivity)? How can expanding our emphasis on this process enhance student achievement?
2. How can we help each student demonstrate viable and effective decision-making skills? How can emphasizing this process enhance our students' sense of intellectual challenge?
3. What research-based instructional strategies can we emphasize to promote a higher level of intellectual challenge for every student? How will this expanded emphasis affect student achievement and motivation?
4. How can we develop and implement observational criteria to determine levels of intellectual challenge in each classroom in our school? How will this process affect school climate and student motivation?
5. What are the consequences of boredom and lethargy for individual students? How can addressing these problems strategically enhance students' sense of motivation and intellectual challenge?
6. To what extent do we contribute to each student's sense of intellectual challenge—or lack of intellectual challenge? How can personalizing our approach to this issue improve student motivation and sense of efficacy?
7. How effectively does our school provide access for every student to rigorous programs in all content areas, including the arts, foreign language, and social studies? How will formal program evaluation in these areas contribute to students' intellectual challenge and motivation?
8. To what extent have we achieved consensus about what constitutes intellectual rigor in our classrooms and school? How can delineating criteria for intellectual challenge within specific content or grade levels and monitoring their levels of implementation enhance student motivation?
9. How can we help each of our students demonstrate prosocial behaviors? How can direct instruction in this area reduce incidents of antisocial behavior?
10. How can we help each student to use the habit of self-regulation? How will this expanded emphasis affect student performance?
11. How can we help each of our students to seek help when necessary to resolve problems? How will this expanded emphasis contribute to students' sense of physical and emotional safety and well-being?
12. How can we support each student to demonstrate prosocial behavior? How will expanding our emphasis in this area contribute to students' sense of personal and emotional safety in our school?
13. How can we improve our monitoring of the physical and emotional safety of classrooms in our school? How will an expanded emphasis in this area affect staff and student productivity?
14. To what extent are we in consensus about what it means for classrooms to be emotionally safe for the instructor and students? How can we enhance our level of agreement in this area? How will this process affect student motivation and staff performance?
15. How can we improve our efficiency and effectiveness in reducing or eliminating incidents of physical threats, incipient violence, and bullying? How can this improvement process enhance students' sense of physical and emotional safety?

16. To what extent are our school buildings, grounds, and vehicles secure? To what extent do they meet all established safety and environmental standards? How can expanding our focus in this area enhance school climate and student performance?
17. To what extent is our school's physical plant attractive and structurally sound, with good internal (hallways) and external (pedestrian and motor vehicle) traffic flow? How can improving our emphasis on these elements enhance staff morale and student motivation?
18. How can we improve our efficiency in identifying and addressing defects in internal and external physical plant structures, resources, and processes? How will expanded emphasis in this area contribute to staff morale and student motivation?
19. To what extent are all school staff, students, and family members in consensus about behavioral expectations, rules, and routines? How can we improve our aggregate and disaggregated performance data in this area? What impact might this process have upon student motivation and sense of physical and emotional safety?
20. How can we ensure that families feel welcomed by school staff as partners in their children's education? How will enhancing our work in this area affect student motivation and achievement?
21. How can schoolwide programs and practices promote social and emotional learning? How will this process affect students' physical and emotional safety?

TENET THREE TOOLS

Ensuring Active Student Engagement and Connectedness

INTRODUCTION 127

TITLE OF TOOL

1. Exploring Key Criteria Associated with Tenet Three. 129

2. Examining Research-Based Best Practices for Tenet Three 131

3–5: Planning and Implementing Professional Development for Tenet Three. 135

    3. A Suggested Agenda for Your Tenet Three Professional Development Activities 136

    4. What Do We Know About Engaging Learning Environments?—Rules of Engagement: A Professional Development Walk-Through Activity 137

    5. What Do We Know About Connected Learning Environments?—A Give-One, Get-One Walkabout Activity 139

6. Study Group Articles and Discussion Questions 145

7. Inquiry Team and Action Research Questions 147

Tenet Three

Ensuring Active Student Engagement and Connectedness

Introduction

Research shows that academic, civic, health, and behavior benefits accrue when students are actively engaged in learning and connected to the school and broader community. This section will help educators and community members to address two primary goals related to these priority areas: (1) to ensure that each student is engaged in the learning process as a result of curriculum, assessment, and instruction that promotes active student involvement; and (2) to ensure that each student experiences a sense of connectedness to their classroom, school, and community.

Students' feelings of engagement, support, and connectedness to family, school, and peers are highly associated with positive health and behaviors. Connections to supportive adults and systems correlates with students' achievement and sense of well-being. In the report *Core Principles for Engaging Young People in Community Change* (Pittman, Martin, & Williams, 2007, p. 6), the authors state that youth contributing to communities and communities contributing to youth result in a powerful interdependence that "create[s] the necessary conditions for the successful development of themselves, their peers, their families and their communities."

The authors describe effective educational program development that incorporates youth engagement as follows:

- Designs an outreach strategy
- Creates a "home base"
- Conveys an intentional philosophy
- Identifies core issues
- Creates youth/adult teams
- Builds youth and adult capacity
- Provides individual supports
- Sustains access and influence

In "A case for school connectedness" (*Educational Leadership* (2005, April),16–20), researcher Robert Blum notes that across disciplines, three school characteristics stand out for helping students feel connected while encouraging student achievement:

- High academic standards coupled with strong teacher support
- An environment in which adult and student relationships are positive and respectful
- A physically and emotionally safe school environment

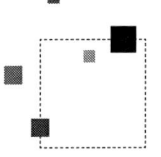

Action Tool One: Exploring Key Criteria Associated with Tenet Three

PURPOSE OF THIS TOOL

Tenet Three in the Whole Child Compact emphasizes the need for every child to experience education as engaging and to be connected to both the school and the community. This tool introduces participants to recommendations and processes that achieve the goals of helping students to experience engagement and connectedness.

HOW TO USE THIS TOOL

Use this tool for stakeholder discussions and for examining classroom practices that affect students' experience of engagement and connectedness. This tool can be used in a variety of venues to establish stakeholder consensus about the status of instructional and assessment practices that support Whole Child education—and areas in which immediate and long-term work may need to occur to enhance students' sense of intellectual, emotional, and social-relational engagement and connectedness.

The ideas and strategies presented can improve student and adult perceptions of how the curriculum connects to the world beyond the classroom. Authentic learning plays a major role in promoting student understanding and students' acquisition of 21st century workplace competencies and habits of mind, a precursor to Tenet Five.

TIPS AND VARIATIONS

✓ Use the materials and activities included to focus study group participants' understanding of the major structural components associated with Whole Child practices related to this tenet.

Exploring Key Criteria Associated with Tenet Three

DIRECTIONS:

- Distribute copies of two Educational Leadership articles available in electronic format as part of this publication:
  R. W. Blum. (2005). A case for school connectedness. *Educational Leadership, 62*(7), 16–20.
  Gail Thompson (March 2008). Beneath the apathy. *Educational Leadership, 65*(6), 50–54.
- Divide into groups of four. Two people in each group read the first article; the other two read the second article.
- After reading the articles, each person takes turns sharing what they learned in the article.
- Using the information from the articles, the whole group discusses and charts answers to the following questions: What do we already have in place in our school? What might we need to change?

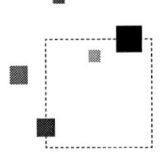

Action Tool Two: Examining Research-Based Best Practices for Tenet Three

PURPOSE OF THIS TOOL

Tenet Three emphasizes two key elements of a positive and productive Whole Child school: student engagement and connectedness to the school and community. This tool uses factors from a synthesis of the research that confirms the close alignment between engagement, connectedness, and positive outcomes for students.

HOW TO USE THIS TOOL

Use this tool to inform your strategic planning process for Tenet Three. It can also be used to provide background knowledge about Tenet Three and to develop consensus about needs and priorities and the ways in which members of the community can help you work on reinforcing student-school and student-community connectedness.

TIPS AND VARIATIONS

- ✓ Continue to emphasize the alignment and interrelationships among the various Whole Child tenets. For example, how do your results from using this action tool align with your commitments to intellectual rigor—and the focus areas you will investigate in Tenet Four (especially personalizing the learning environment) and Tenet Five (preparing every student for postsecondary education and the 21st century workplace)?
- ✓ Use the ideas and strategies presented here as a springboard for potential cross-institutional partnership work. Partnerships can be especially beneficial when you are considering changes in curriculum content, uses of technology, and related ways to promote engagement and connectedness.
- ✓ Share your conclusions and recommendations with your school improvement or district strategic planning team(s) to reinforce effective collaboration and a seamless, holistic approach to school reform and transformation.

Examining Research-Based Best Practices for Tenet Three

Directions: Use this tool as a data collection form to gather information for your strategic action plan. Ask participants to complete the matrix individually. Display ratings on chart paper for all to see. Use the results to develop priorities for action planning.

As you consider the skills, competencies, and recommended practices, rate your school or district on the extent to which each plays a key part in each student's education:

4 = High degree of evidence; 3 = Adequate degree of evidence; 2 = Some degree of evidence, but needs further attention; 1 = No evidence with major need for attention and emphasis.

Part I: Student Behaviors	Rating
1. The student self-manages his or her own learning process.	4 3 2 1
2. The student displays energy about and commitment to the learning process.	4 3 2 1
3. The student exhibits a sense of purpose and authenticity, articulating real-world connections between school experiences and his or her life experiences.	4 3 2 1
4. Each student feels connected to the school and experiences him- or herself as part of a learning community.	4 3 2 1
Research-Based Organizational Practices (School Level)	**Rating**
1. Teachers use active learning strategies such as cooperative learning and project-based learning:	
• All instructors clearly communicate to students the content and performance standards for which they are responsible.	4 3 2 1
• Teachers work closely with students to help them monitor their own progress based on clearly articulated levels of performance (e.g., beginning, basic, proficient, advanced).	4 3 2 1
• Students are encouraged to celebrate their own success as they progress toward standards-based achievement.	4 3 2 1
• All instructors engage student interest through experience-based introductory activities designed to expose them to new declarative (i.e., information) and procedural (i.e., skills and procedures) knowledge.	4 3 2 1
• Teachers use a range of inquiry-based, experiential learning tasks and activities to help all students deepen their understanding of what they are learning and why they are learning it.	4 3 2 1
2. Instructors use a range of diagnostic, formative, and summative assessment tasks to monitor student progress, provide timely feedback, and adjust teaching-learning activities to maximize student progress:	
• Curriculum is anchored around benchmark performance assessment tasks, including academic prompts and culminating projects.	4 3 2 1

Research-Based Organizational Practices (School Level) (continued)	Rating
3. The school provides each student with an adult advisor or mentor:	
• Adult advisors ensure that every student has a significant adult within the school building to encourage and support his or her progress.	4 3 2 1
• Mentors are in place for every student, ensuring that appropriate coaching and counseling are present to support academic and personal growth.	4 3 2 1
4. The school culture is conducive to making students and staff members feel accepted and valued.	4 3 2 1
5. The school offers professional development, coaching, and mentoring to teachers to ensure that	
• Teachers emphasize and model mutual respect for all persons in their classrooms.	4 3 2 1
• Teachers support and have high expectations for all students.	4 3 2 1
• Teachers treat all students fairly, consistently, and uniformly.	4 3 2 1
• Teachers promote students' use of cooperative learning skills.	4 3 2 1
6. The school expects students to assume age-appropriate responsibility for learning through effective decision making, goal setting, and time management.	4 3 2 1
7. The school has access to school counselors or other student support systems:	
• An appropriate student-counselor ratio is operational to ensure that every student can access counseling programs and resources, as needed.	4 3 2 1
• School counselors ensure that all students understand requirements for college, university, and related postsecondary educational options.	4 3 2 1
• Counselors work with each student to ensure appropriate preparation for the world of work, including interest surveys, aptitude profiles, and monitoring of graduation requirements.	4 3 2 1
• The school's counseling program ensures that every student has access to needed health and human services.	4 3 2 1
8. The school offers a range of opportunities for students to contribute to the community at large, including service projects and evidence-based service learning.	4 3 2 1
9. The school is structured to reinforce ethical citizenship behaviors by students and staff, including meaningful participation in decision making in the classroom and at the school level.	4 3 2 1
10. The school provides opportunities for community-based apprenticeships, internships, and projects:	
• Enrichment experiences complement available extracurricular activities and programs to ensure that all students have a range of options for enhancing their academic background knowledge.	4 3 2 1
11. Curriculum-related experiences such as field trips, outreach projects, and related forms of activity complement and extend students' in-class learning activities.	4 3 2 1

Research-Based Organizational Practices (School Level) (continued)	Rating
12. The school offers a wide array of extracurricular activities:	
• Extracurricular programs and activities offer students a range of options and choices designed to accommodate diverse goals, interests, and learning profiles.	4 3 2 1
13. Extracurricular programs and activities reinforce students' self-esteem, emotional intelligence, and sense of efficacy.	4 3 2 1

Research-Based Organizational Practices (District, Community, State and Federal Government)	Rating
Our local school district	
• Develops student-centered academic plans and a process for students to provide input throughout their academic careers.	4 3 2 1
• Ensures a full complement of extracurricular activities.	4 3 2 1
• Develops processes for student participation in schoolwide decision making and governance.	4 3 2 1
Our community	
• Collaborates with school districts to provide learning opportunities in both schools and the community.	4 3 2 1
• Helps schools develop extracurricular and after-school activities that incorporate community experiences.	4 3 2 1
• Provides opportunities for community-based learning through apprenticeships with local businesses.	4 3 2 1

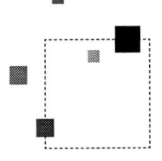

Action Tools Three–Five: Planning and Implementing Professional Development for Tenet Three

PURPOSE OF THESE TOOLS

This set of action tools will help your team design and implement professional development activities to support your Tenet Three work.

HOW TO USE THE TOOLS

Determine which tools match the needs of the group with which you will be using them. Customize the professional development activities aligned with the needs and goals of the group.

Included with these Tenet Three professional development action tools are the following resources and materials:

1. A Suggested Agenda for Your Tenet Three Professional Development Activities
2. What Do We Know About Engaging Learning Environments?
3. What Do We Know About Connected Learning Environments?

TIPS AND VARIATIONS

✓ Determine if you wish to develop and implement a Tenet Three–specific professional development program involving initial staff orientation sessions to ensure a common understanding and knowledge base.
✓ Invite members of your student support team and other school teams to participate in study groups.

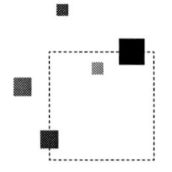

Action Tool Three: A Suggested Agenda for Your Tenet Three Professional Development Activities

Objectives: Participants will be able to—

- Explore and understand the key principles and recommended practices associated with Tenet Three of the Whole Child Compact: (1) ensuring active student engagement, and (2) helping each student to feel connected to the school and the community.
- Examine their own work with students and themselves in relationship to promoting Tenet Three priorities.
- Make recommendations for areas in which they and the school might improve identified Tenet Three priorities.

Suggested Professional Development Activities and Related Action Tools:

- What Do We Know About Engaging Learning Environments? (Rules of Engagement: A Professional Development Walk-Through Activity)
- What Do We Know About Connected Learning Environments? (A Give-One, Get-One Walkabout Activity)

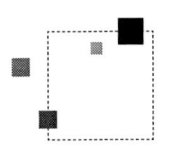

Action Tool Four: What Do We Know About Engaging Learning Environments?—Rules of Engagement: A Professional Development Walk-Through Activity

DIRECTIONS:

1. This activity engages participants in an imaginary walk-through activity. You will need several video examples of classroom episodes representing a variety of areas (5–10 minutes per episode).
2. Participants will form walk-through teams. They will be responsible for "moving" from classroom to classroom, applying the criteria identified below from Robert Marzano's text, *The Art and Science of Teaching.*
3. Ideally, television monitors can be set up throughout a large training room as viewing centers. As in a real walk-through, the team will attempt to go in and out of as many classrooms as possible. If multiple monitors are not available, the entire training group can watch the series of short classroom episodes and then complete their team reports.
4. Reports should be a combination of bulleted notes on flipchart pages and an oral summary of what the team members observed in response to three major questions related to "the rules of engagement": (a) How engaged in learning were students in each classroom we observed? (b) What were the signs of engagement we can identify (e.g., high energy, activities involving missing information, activation of the self-system)? (c) What commendations and recommendations would we make?

Robert J. Marzano:
What the Research Tells Us About Student Engagement

(Research conclusions presented by Dr. Robert J. Marzano in his 2007 ASCD text, *The Art and Science of Teaching.*)

1. Engagement is reflected in on-task behavior combined with students' emotions, cognition, and voice. According to Reeve (2006, cited on p. 99 of Marzano's text), "When engagement is characterized by the full range of on-task behavior, positive emotions, invested cognition, and personal voice, it functions as the engine for learning and development."
2. Marzano cites five major areas in which teachers can increase student engagement (pp. 100–103):

- High energy: boosted by physical activity, instructional pacing, and teacher enthusiasm.
- Working with missing information: engaging students in working with puzzles and games that activate the phenomenon of "clozentropy," the impulse to lessen the discrepancy between what someone predicts will occur and what is actually occurring.
- Activating all aspects of the "self-system": involving students in activities that touch on or activate what is important to them at their core, that is, what they find increasingly valuable and interesting.
- Using mild pressure to stimulate engagement: nonthreatening but interesting activities in which mild pressure is present to increase levels of engagement. Unpredictable questioning patterns, for example, can increase levels of attention and engagement.
- Incorporating mild controversy and competition: activities such as structured debates to increase student engagement and interest without threatening the learner. Similarly, games in which students compete in teams can also enhance engagement.

How Engaging Were the Classrooms You Observed?

1. Examples of student behaviors reflecting engagement:

2. Examples of teacher behaviors that encouraged engagement:

3. Examples in which engagement was weak or missing:

4. Commendations:

5. Recommendations:

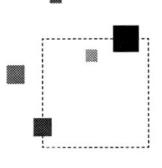

Action Tool Five: What Do We Know About Connected Learning Environments? A Give-One, Get-One Walkabout Activity

DIRECTIONS:

1. This professional development activity involves the strategy of "giving one to get one." In this case, participants will have the opportunity to process a great deal of research information about the relationship between connectedness (i.e., the student feeling connected to teachers, classrooms, school, and the community) and levels of student engagement. As you will see, the two conditions are closely linked in the studies presented below.
2. Ask each participant to read and reflect on one (or more) of the seven selections presented in this resource tool and record their thoughts on the following questions: What do the research authors suggest about ways schools can connect students with their learning environment? How do the strategies they present support and enhance student engagement in the learning process?
3. At the end of the reflection period (10–15 minutes), participants should get up and do a "walkabout" in which they share an insight or conclusion from what they have read with a partner who did not read their selection. During these brief interactions (two to three minutes), partners should begin to discuss areas of commonality and parallel insights found in the readings.
4. At the conclusion of the give-one, get-one walkabout, participants should return to their original seats. At that point, the facilitator should help the group synthesize their conclusions and insights. What have we learned about connected students, classrooms, and schools?

Selection One

The National Research Council Institute of Medicine of the National Academies report, *Engaging Schools: Fostering High School Students' Motivation to Learn* (Institute of Medicine, 2004, p. 2), asserts, "A common theme among effective practices is that they address underlying psychological variables related to motivation, such as competence and control, beliefs about the value of education, and a sense of belonging. In brief, engaging schools and teachers promote students' confidence in their ability to learn and succeed in school by providing challenging instruction and support for meeting high standards, and they clearly convey their own high expectations for their students' success." The report contains such specific recommendations as the following:

- High school courses and instructional methods should be redesigned in ways that will increase adolescent engagement and learning.
- There should be ongoing classroom-based assessment of students' understanding and skills.
- Preservice teacher preparation programs should provide high school teachers deep content knowledge and a range of pedagogical strategies and understandings about adolescents and how they learn. Schools and districts should provide practicing teachers with opportunities to work with colleagues and to continue to develop their skills.
- Schools should provide the support and resources necessary to help all high school students to meet challenging standards.

- Tests used to evaluate schools, teachers, and students should assess high-level, critical thinking and incorporate broad and multidimensional conceptions of subject matter, including fluency, conceptual understanding, analysis, and application.
- Districts should restructure comprehensive urban high schools to create smaller learning communities that foster personalized and continuous relationships between teachers and students.
- Both formal and informal tracking by ability should be eliminated. Alternative strategies should be used to ensure appropriately challenging instruction for students who vary widely in their skill levels.
- School guidance and counseling responsibilities should be diffused among school staff, including teachers, who are supported by professionals.
- Efforts should be made to improve communication, coordination, and trust among the adults in the various settings where adolescents spend their time. These settings include homes, religious institutions, and the various organized extracurricular activities sponsored by schools and community groups.
- Schools should make greater efforts to identify and coordinate with social and health services in the community, and policy makers should revise policies to facilitate students' access to the services they need.

Selection Two

R. Blum (2005) in *School Connectedness: Improving Students' Lives* identifies seven qualities in schools that promote high levels of student engagement and attachment: having a sense of belonging and being part of a school, liking school, perceiving that teachers are supportive and caring, having good friends within school, being engaged in their own current and future academic progress, believing that discipline is fair and effective, and participating in extracurricular activities. Blum recommends the following school connectedness strategies:

- Implement high standards and expectations, and provide academic support to all students.
- Apply fair and consistent disciplinary policies that are collectively agreed upon and fairly enforced.
- Create trusting relationships among students, teachers, staff, administrators, and families.
- Hire and support capable teachers who are skilled in content, teaching techniques, and classroom management to meet each learner's needs.
- Foster high parent/family expectations for school performance and school completion.
- Ensure that every student feels close to at least one supportive adult at school.

Selection Three

The issue of engagement and relatedness is an extraordinarily important one in sustaining students' commitment to completing their education—and thus supporting dropout prevention. Once again, this critical factor reinforces the interrelationships among the various tenets of the Whole Child Initiative. In *Engaged for Success: Service-Learning as a Tool for High School Dropout Prevention,* for example, Bridgeland, Dilulio, and Wulsin (2008) cite the following statistics:

- Eighty-two percent of students who participate in service learning and 80 percent of at-risk students not in service learning programs say their feelings about attending high school became or would become more positive as a result of service learning.

- More than 75 percent of all students, including current and past students in service learning programs and at-risk students who did not participate in service learning, agree that service learning classes are more interesting than other classes.
- Forty-five percent of service learning students and 38 percent of at-risk students who were not in service learning programs believe service learning classes are more worthwhile than other classes.
- Seventy-seven percent of students in service learning programs and 66 percent of at-risk students who did not participate in service learning programs say that service learning had or would have had a big effect on motivating them to work hard.
- Seventy-four percent of African Americans, 70 percent of Hispanics, and 64 percent of all students said that service learning could have a big effect on keeping students in school.

Selection Four

The commitment to engaging student learning also aligns powerfully with promoting a sense of ethical citizenship among students. The publication *Restoring the Balance Between Academics and Civic Engagement in Public Schools* (American Youth Policy Forum & Association for Supervision and Curriculum Development, 2005) offers seven propositions to increase civic engagement through school activities:

- The business of public education in America is and should be to teach young people how to take charge of their own learning and to become responsible, informed, and engaged citizens.
- We must sharpen the mission of our schools to make sure it includes the knowledge, dispositions, virtues, and skills of responsible citizenship.
- Civic knowledge—learning how the community works—and civic engagement—the practice of becoming effective in that process—must become integral to a broadened "core" of learning.
- Civic education, which includes the methodologies of service learning and character education, has demonstrated success in improving student engagement in school and community life, bolstering academic performance, and reducing negative behaviors.
- Realign education reform efforts to support opportunities of integrated curricula.
- An action plan is required to accomplish the mission outlined in this report. The plan should provide a clear path for educators to link academic subjects with service learning and character education, or other strategies, in support of greater civic knowledge and engagement experiences for students.
- Success in all these approaches should be grounded in a collaborative effort that links community resources—schools, families, higher education, community organizations, philanthropic organizations, local government, and the business and nonprofit sectors—in support of student success in civic learning and civic engagement.

Selection Five

From Pearson (2002) and Fletcher (2005):
When is student involvement meaningful?

- When students are allies and partners with adults in improving schools.

- When students have the training and authority to create real solutions to the challenges that schools face in learning, teaching, and leadership.
- When schools, including educators and administrators, are accountable to the direct consumers of schools—students themselves.
- When student-adult partnerships are a major component of every sustainable, responsive, and systemic approach to transforming schools.

When is student involvement not meaningful?

- When students are regarded as passive recipients in schools, or as empty vessels to be filled with teachers' knowledge.
- When the contributions of students are minimized or tokenized by adults by asking students to "rubber stamp" ideas developed by adults, or by inviting students to sit on committees without real power or responsibility.
- When student perspectives, experiences, or knowledge are filtered with adult interpretations.
- When students are given problems to solve without adult support or adequate training; or students are trained in leadership skills without opportunities to take on real leadership roles in their school.

Selection Six

Schools and communities committed to educating the whole child foster engagement with and a sense of connection for students to the school community. Together they provide a variety of opportunities for meaningful student involvement, interest-based activities, and personalized responses to students' learning needs. Often these opportunities are framed through experiential learning that allows young people to practice the skills, knowledge, and behaviors required for participation in society.

In 2003, the Center for Adolescent Health and Development at the University of Minnesota, the Centers for Disease Control and Prevention's Division of Adolescent and School Health, and the Johnson Foundation convened a conference that teamed researchers in the health and education sectors with government and non-governmental agency representatives to develop a core set of principles to guide schools on issues of school connectedness. Their statement, "Wingspread Declaration on School Connections" (2004), included five core elements:

- Student success increases through strengthened bonds with school.
- Students feel connected when they experience high expectations for academic success, feel supported by staff, and feel safe in their school.
- School connectedness affects critical accountability measures, such as academic performance, fighting, truancy, and dropout rates.
- School connectedness increases educational motivation, classroom engagement, and attendance, which can then be linked to higher academic achievement.
- School connectedness can lower rates of disruptive behavior, substance and tobacco use, emotional distress, and early age of first sex.

Selection Seven

Meaningful student involvement in school includes opportunities to provide leadership, engage in decision making, and participate in planning learning experiences. It reinforces critical thinking, active problem solving, civic participation, and an appreciation for diverse opinions. Schools and communities that foster meaningful student involvement support organized student participation in educational decision making, planning, research, and advocacy, and the integration of such activities into daily curricular and instructional practices (Fletcher, 2003).

Other performance indicators associated with Tenet Three are taken from the literature on connectedness and from H. Jerome Freiberg's (2003) *School Climate: Measuring, Improving, and Sustaining Healthy Learning Environments* (London: RoutledgeFalmer) theories on the importance of school climate. For example, a healthy school supports a physical school environment with buildings, grounds, and vehicles that are secure and meet all established safety and environmental standards. Similarly, a comprehensive crisis management and response system is in place and plays a sustained, active role in promoting a safe and orderly learning environment.

A key originating point for this tenet involved the "Wingspread Declaration on School Connections" (2004). This declaration is based on a detailed review of research and in-depth discussions among an interdisciplinary group of educational leaders convened at Wingspread, June 13–15, 2003. According to the Wingspread Declaration,

1. Students are more likely to succeed when they feel connected to school. Critical requirements for feeling connected include students' experiencing

   - High academic expectations and rigor coupled with support for learning
   - Positive adult-student relationships
   - Safety—both physical and emotional

2. Based on current research evidence, the most effective strategies for increasing the likelihood that students will be connected to school include

   - Implementing high standards and expectations, and providing academic support to all students
   - Applying fair and consistent disciplinary policies that are collectively agreed upon and fairly enforced
   - Creating trusting relationships among students, teachers, staff, administrators, and families
   - Hiring and supporting capable teachers skilled in content, teaching techniques, and classroom management to meet each learner's needs
   - Fostering high parent/family expectations for school performance and school completion
   - Ensuring that every student feels close to at least one supportive adult at school

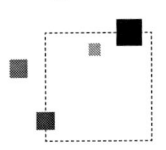

Action Tool Six: Study Group Articles and Discussion Questions

PURPOSE OF THIS TOOL

This tool provides suggestions for *Educational Leadership* articles in electronic format for use in your Tenet Three study groups. The electronic articles are available for download at www.ascd.org/downloads.

HOW TO USE THIS TOOL

Refer to the study guideline and tools included in the Overview section to support the planning and implementation of your study group.

Study Group Articles and Discussion Questions

1. **Nel Noddings (2008, February). All our students thinking.** *Educational Leadership, 65*(5), 8–13.

   - What are the characteristics of teaching that is intellectually challenging to the student? How do these characteristics contribute to engaged student learning?
   - How can learning as exploration enhance students' sense of engagement?
   - Informal and nonthreatening competition has been identified as a factor in promoting student engagement while learning. What does Noddings suggest about this practice?

2. **Donna Marie San Antonio (2008, April). Understanding students' strengths and struggles.** *Educational Leadership, 65*(7), 74–79.

   - Why does San Antonio suggest that the two identified processes be an essential part of effective schools and classrooms?
   - How do school relationships contribute to students' sense of connection to their school and community?
   - Describe the relationship between knowing students and knowing their communities.
   - How can San Antonio's recommendations in this article support your Whole Child strategic planning process?

3. **Andrea Sobel & Eileen Gale Kugler (2007, March). Building partnerships with immigrant parents.** *Educational Leadership, 64*(6), 62–66.

   - What are the key elements of the parent outreach program described in this article?
   - In your opinion, to what extent does this program "transcend traditional approaches," as described by the authors?
   - How can the parent outreach and resources presented in this article support your efforts to ensure that each student is connected to his or her school and community?

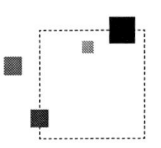

Action Tool Seven: Inquiry Team and Action Research Questions

PURPOSE OF THIS TOOL

This tool will support your planning process for the tenet and also guide implementation and evaluation of what is working.

HOW TO USE THIS TOOL

Determine which questions are aligned with your school community's needs and goals. Use the inquiry and action research tools included in the Overview section to guide your work.

TIPS AND VARIATIONS

✓ Have small groups elect three to five different inquiry or action research questions as a focus area. Share plans and actions resulting from discussions and action research results in ongoing learning community meetings.

Inquiry Team and Action Research Questions

Tenet Three Inquiry Focus Questions

1. To what extent does each student successfully manage his or her own learning process? How do we know?
2. To what extent does each student consistently display energy and commitment to the learning process?
3. What barriers or problems lead to boredom or disengagement in our classrooms?
4. How well does each student demonstrate a sense of purpose and authenticity about their learning process?
5. How effectively can each learner articulate real-world connections between school experiences and his or her life experiences?
6. To what extent does each student demonstrate positive attitudes toward school?
7. How effectively and consistently do we monitor students' attitude toward learning?
8. To what extent does each student demonstrate an understanding of the relationship between the school and the community?
9. How frequently do our students display behaviors that contribute to the community at large?
10. How do we monitor our students' connections with their community?
11. To what extent does each student display behaviors associated with ethical citizenship (e.g., commitment to civic discourse; valuing a balance of rights and responsibilities; participation in decision-making processes; respect for the rule of law; appropriate questioning of authority, policies, and regulations)?
12. To what extent is each actively engaged in learning and connected to the school and broader community? How do we know?
13. How effectively do our school and classrooms offer students opportunities to develop lifelong intellectual dispositions (i.e., "habits of mind" such as metacognition, self-regulation, critical thinking, and creativity)?
14. How frequently does each teacher use active learning strategies such as cooperative learning and project-based learning? How do we monitor this use?
15. To what extent does each student feel connected to the school, experiencing himself or herself as part of a vital and interesting learning community?
16. Does the school provide each student with an adult advisor or mentor? How do we monitor and assess the impact of such advisory experiences?
17. To what extent is our school culture conducive to making students and staff members feel accepted and valued?
18. How effectively does our school offer professional development, coaching, and mentoring to teachers to ensure that their instructional practices are engaging and research based?
19. To what extent does our school include students in the establishment of routines, rules, and behavioral expectations at the classroom and school levels?
20. To what extent do we expect all students to assume age-appropriate responsibility for learning through effective decision making, goal setting, and time management?
21. To what extent does each student have access to school counselors or other student support systems? How do we evaluate the impact and value added of these services?
22. Does our school offer a range of opportunities for students to contribute to the community at large, including service projects and service learning aligned with curriculum standards and priorities?

23. To what extent is the school structured and organized to support learning?
24. Does our school provide opportunities for each student to participate in community-based apprenticeships, internships, and service-related projects? How do we determine the impact of such learning activities?
25. How do curriculum-related experiences such as field trips, outreach projects, and related forms of activity complement and extend students' in-class learning activities?
26. To what extent does the school offer a wide array of extracurricular activities? How do these activities affect students' sense of engagement and connectedness?
27. To what extent do extracurricular programs and activities reinforce students' self-esteem, emotional intelligence, and sense of efficacy?

Action Research Questions for Tenet Three
1. How will expanding our emphasis on strategies to help each student manage his or her own learning process successfully enhance student motivation and performance?
2. How will applying research-based strategies for promoting student energy and commitment to learning affect our aggregate and disaggregated student achievement results?
3. How can building consensus about and applying strategies to alleviate boredom or disengagement in our classrooms affect student engagement and motivation?
4. How can we expand each student's sense of purpose and authenticity in relationship to their learning process? How will this expansion affect achievement results?
5. How can asking each learner to articulate real-world connections between school experiences and his or her life experiences enhance engagement, motivation, and achievement?
6. How can we work with students to identify and reinforce positive attitudes toward learning and to school? How will formalizing our approach to this issue impact student achievement data?
7. What does research suggest about helping students to feel connected to their school? How will implementing one or more of these strategies affect student motivation, engagement, and achievement?
8. How can we develop and implement curriculum enhancements to reinforce student understanding of relationships between their school and their community? What effects will this process have on student engagement, motivation, and achievement?
9. How will expanding our emphasis on helping students to make contributions to the community at large affect student motivation and performance?
10. How do we monitor our students' connections with their community? How can enhancing this process help to make students feel more connected to their school, community, and education? How can we tell?
11. What does it mean for our students to become ethical citizens? How can emphasizing one or more of the following in our curriculum and instructional activities enhance student connectedness to the school and community? Areas for action research emphasis might include (a) commitment to civic discourse; (b) valuing a balance of rights and responsibilities; (c) participation in decision-making processes; (d) respect for the rule of law; (e) appropriate questioning of authority, policies, and regulations.
12. How can expanding our school and classroom emphasis on students' development of lifelong intellectual dispositions (i.e., "habits of mind" such as metacognition, self-regulation, critical thinking, and creativity) enhance student engagement and connectedness to learning?

13. How will expanded instructional emphasis on active learning strategies such as cooperative learning and project-based learning affect student motivation and achievement?
14. How can we collaborate to support each of our students to feel connected to the school, experiencing himself or herself as part of a vital and interesting learning community? How will this process affect student engagement and motivation?
15. How can we expand student access to adult advisors or mentors? How can we monitor and assess the impact of such advisory experiences?
16. How can we improve our school's professional development, coaching, and mentoring to teachers to ensure that their instructional practices are engaging and research based? How will enhancing these processes improve student engagement and connectedness to learning?
17. To what extent does our school include students in the establishment of routines, rules, and behavioral expectations at the classroom and school levels? How will expanding our emphasis in this area improve students' sense of engagement and connectedness to the school?
18. How will enhancing students' understanding and application of decision making, goal setting, and time management skills and processes affect their sense of engagement and connectedness to learning?
19. How can we improve student access to counseling programs and other student support systems? How will this expansion affect student achievement and motivation?
20. How will expanding opportunities for students to contribute to the community at large (e.g., service projects and service learning aligned with curriculum standards and priorities) promote student engagement and connectedness to the school and community?
21. How will expanding the range of curriculum-related field experiences (e.g., field trips, outreach projects, and related forms of activity) enhance student engagement and connectedness?
22. How can we expand each student's participation in extracurricular activities? How will this expansion affect their motivation, engagement, and connectedness?

TENET FOUR TOOLS

Personalizing the Learning Process and Ensuring That All Learners Work with Qualified, Caring Adults

INTRODUCTION 153

TITLE OF TOOL

1. Exploring Key Criteria Associated with Tenet Four 155

2. Examining Your School's Current Status—Strategies for Data Collection and Analysis for Tenet Four 157

3. Examining Research-Based Best Practices for Tenet Four 159

4–7: Planning and Implementing Professional Development for Tenet Four 163

    4. A Suggested Agenda for Your Tenet Four Professional Development Activities 164

    5. What Is a Personalized Approach to Learning? 165

    6. Investigating Criteria for Ensuring That Each Student Works with Qualified, Caring Adults 168

    7. Implementing and Sustaining Effective Student Advisories, Mentoring Programs, Counseling, and Related Student Support Systems 170

8. Study Group Articles and Discussion Questions 173

9. Inquiry Team and Action Research Questions 175

Personalizing the Learning Process and Ensuring That All Learners Work with Qualified, Caring Adults

Introduction

This module will help educators, families, community members, and other stakeholders to address two primary goals: (1) to ensure that the learning process is personalized for each student; and (2) to ensure that each student works with qualified, caring adults. In the face of increasingly complex demands from postsecondary educational institutions as well as the workplace of the 21st century, ensuring that schools are safe, orderly, and inviting learning communities is essential. The pathways toward achieving this vision involve differentiation of curriculum, assessment, and instruction as well as ensuring that each student works with adults who are both caring and professionally qualified.

The core components of personalized learning (often referred to as pastoral learning in countries outside the United States) include the development of individualized learning plans designed to inspire students' enthusiasm for their studies but also to keep them on the path toward earning a high school diploma. Personalized learning measures recognize the intellectual capacity, interests, and aspirations unique to each student; the involvement of students in decision making regarding their academic life; and the appointment of dedicated advisors and mentors for each student.

ASCD calls for personalized learning initiatives that encourage students' sense of ownership over their own educational activities and promote their appreciation of the connection between their learning and their future goals. These initiatives will enable students not only to perceive greater relevance in their schoolwork, but also to grow increasingly engaged in school, connected to adults, and prepared for graduation and future success.

In addition, through interactions with responsive, respectful adults—regardless of their role within a child's life—children learn to imitate, and then internalize, valued social, physical, cognitive, or ethical behaviors. When children believe that the adults around them care about who they are, what they know, and what they can do, they are more likely to respond to what those adults value and take those values as their own. If there is a cohesive thread among each of the studies, reports, and examples we have cited thus far, it is the influence of positive, respectful, supportive relationships between students and adults within the school and community:

- Wingspread Declaration on School Connections: Positive adult-student relationships are critical for student connectedness.
- Learning First Alliance: We learn best from those with whom we are in caring, mutually respectful relationships that promote independence.
- California Department of Education: Most important in determining the school environment is the quality of students' relationships with other students and with the school's staff.

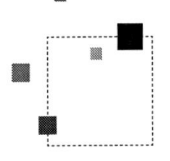

Action Tool One: Exploring Key Criteria Associated with Tenet Four

PURPOSE OF THIS TOOL

Tenet Four of the Whole Child Compact encourages school staffs to personalize the learning environment for every student. It also emphasizes the need for every student to work with qualified and caring adults. This tool introduces participants to the range of recommendations and processes advocated by the Whole Child Compact to achieve the goals of personalization and differentiation as well as issues related to staff certification, content mastery, and affective and social-relational skills and competencies.

HOW TO USE THIS TOOL

This tool offers a rich range of ideas and recommendations for your team's work with Tenet Four. It can be used to facilitate staff discussions concerning key elements of this tenet. Whole Child strategic planning teams may elect to use this tool for stakeholder discussions, including analyzing gaps and omissions in classroom practices that weaken students' experience of intellectual rigor. It can also be used to investigate initial ideas for enhancing the school's current success with personalizing and differentiating the learning environment, as well as attracting and maintaining on staff qualified and caring individuals.

TIPS AND VARIATIONS

- ✓ This tool can be used to support an initial study group involving members of your Whole Child strategic planning team. Use the materials and activities included here to focus members' understanding of the major structural components associated with successful Tenet Four implementation.
- ✓ This tool can also be used with stakeholder sessions dedicated to identifying priorities related to such issues as curriculum mapping and revision, and enhanced emphasis on personalization and differentiation.
- ✓ You can also use the ideas and strategies presented here as part of your work to improve professional development, hiring practices, and preservice training programs.
- ✓ It is especially important in your work on this tenet to involve cross-institutional partners and stakeholder groups. How, for example, can local colleges of education collaborate with your school or district to improve teacher preparation and certification programs? How can you expand the number of board-certified teacher candidates in your school or district?

Exploring Key Criteria Associated with Tenet Four

DIRECTIONS:

Ask key stakeholder groups (e.g., staff, families, students) to organize themselves into groups of five and be ready to respond to the questions below. Provide each group with the list of questions and request that they select four of the eight questions to discuss. They should spend no more than five to seven minutes per question. After each discussion, the group then prepares a quote that summarizes the essence of the dialogue that has occurred. The quotes are then posted. The large group does a gallery walk to observe and take notes of the quotes. The recorder should keep track of participant responses and, at the conclusion of the initial orientation cycle, synthesize response patterns and recommendations extending from this beginning process for Tenet Four.

1. What does it mean for students to experience a personalized learning environment?
2. What should we observe in classrooms when every student experiences a personalized learning environment?
3. What kinds of instructional strategies and techniques would you expect in classrooms with teachers who personalize the learning environment for their students?
4. What does it mean for a staff member to be qualified?
5. How does the term "qualified adult" vary with the individual's roles and responsibilities?
6. What does it mean for an adult to be caring in relationship to students?
7. What are the behaviors we would consider caring in a professional sense?
8. How would you summarize the characteristics of our building and the classrooms in it? To what extent do you believe that all our classrooms are personalized? To what extent does every student appear to work with qualified, caring adults?

What are our conclusions and recommendations in these areas of Tenet Four?

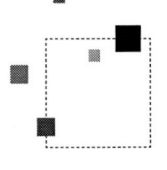

Action Tool Two: Examining Your School's Current Status—Strategies for Data Collection and Analysis for Tenet Four

PURPOSE OF THIS TOOL

As your Whole Child strategic planning team completes its discussion and analysis of Tenet Four programs and practices in your school or district, a next step will be data collection and analysis related to your recommendations. This tool will provide a process for your team to determine how accurate your initial insights and recommendations were, by examining student, staff, and stakeholder data regarding how personalized the learning environment is for every student and how caring and qualified staff members are.

HOW TO USE THIS TOOL

Examine the recommendations presented in this tool. Then, consider the available evidence to determine the extent to which each element or strategy is fully operational. For areas in which there may be insufficient data to allow valid conclusions, consider how your team might acquire those data to make valid inferences and recommendations for program development and school change.

TIPS AND VARIATIONS

- ✓ Use this tool and the analytical processes it generates to determine key elements of your Tenet Four work. For example, who should be the key players in bringing about change and transformation? Who needs to be involved to address Tenet Four gaps and emerging priorities and goals? How can we work more actively with our human resources department to ensure qualified and caring new staff hires? How should we involve the community? How will students be involved in making change occur, including potential service learning projects that can reinforce personalized and differentiated approaches to learning?
- ✓ Use the results to decide what individuals and organizations are missing from your stakeholder groups who can support the changes and resources you will need to personalize the learning environment and ensure that every staff member is qualified and caring.

Examining Your School's Current Status—Strategies for Data Collection and Analysis for Tenet Four

Ask key stakeholder groups (e.g., staff, families, students) to respond to the questions below. They should work in groups of three to five. Each question will be posted on chart paper. Groups will discuss their responses to each question, charting their responses on the paper. After five minutes, each group moves to the next question. After a short discussion, members add their ideas using a different color marker and placing a check mark next to the comments already noted that resonate with their own thinking. After all the questions have been discussed, participants take a walk around the room to view the comments and make notes of ideas and recommendations for the future action planning.

1. How do we personalize the learning process for every student? What sources can help us answer this question?
2. How do we differentiate instruction and assessment to accommodate students' varying readiness levels? What sources can help us answer this question?
3. How do we differentiate instruction and assessment to accommodate every student's learning profile? What sources can help us answer this question?
4. How do we differentiate instruction and assessment to incorporate individual student interests? What sources can help us answer this question?
5. To what extent is each student working with a qualified adult in every classroom? What sources can help us answer this question?
6. To what extent is each student working with a caring adult in every classroom? What sources can help us answer this question?
7. How do we ensure that every adult receives appropriate professional development to sustain his or her knowledge and credentials? What sources can help us answer this question?
8. To what extent do our hiring practices and policies reinforce our ability to have qualified, caring adults working with our students? How do we know?
9. How much evidence do we see of nonteaching adults in our school demonstrating professionalism, caring, and support as they interact with every student?
10. Overall, how personalized is our learning environment for every student? What can we do to improve in this area? Similarly, how qualified and caring is our overall staff? What data sources can help us to explore these issues?

Initial Reflections and Recommendations for Tenet Four:

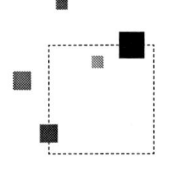

Action Tool Three: Examining Research-Based Best Practices for Tenet Four

PURPOSE OF THIS TOOL

Tenet Four emphasizes student engagement as a key element for success. It also stresses that students must feel connected to their peers, teachers, administrators, overall school, and community if they are to perceive their education as authentic and purposeful. This tool will provide a synthesis of the research that confirms the close alignment between these two factors. It will guide you in examining how a personalized and highly connected learning environment can help students viewed as underachievers.

HOW TO USE THIS TOOL

Use this tool with parent, community, and related stakeholder groups to bring about consensus about where you are heading and why you are going there with various components of Tenet Four. An essential question for this tenet involves student, family, and community feedback on levels of engagement and connectedness for every student.

TIPS AND VARIATIONS

✓ Continue to emphasize the interrelationships between the various Whole Child tenets. For example, how do your results from using this tool align with your commitments to helping each student experience a challenging learning environment that includes real-world applications?

Examining Research-Based Best Practices for Tenet Four

Directions: This matrix can be used in a variety of ways, including (1) observation walk-throughs, (2) initiating community conversations related to this particular tenet, (3) promoting staff discussions of how successfully a school is preparing each student for college and postgraduation study, (4) facilitating stakeholder discussions examining the extent to which a school is successfully preparing each student for work in a global environment, and (5) initial strategic planning for professional development as part of your school improvement planning process.

As you consider the skills, competencies, and recommended practices, rate your school or district on the extent to which each plays a key part in each student's education:

4 = High degree of evidence; 3 = Adequate degree of evidence; 2 = Some degree of evidence, but needs further attention; 1 = Minimum degree of evidence with need for much more attention; 0 = No evidence with major need for attention and emphasis.

Part I: Student Indicators	Rating
The following are research-based student behaviors associated with the key elements of this tenet, including students' experiencing a personalized learning environment and working with qualified, caring adults:	
1. Each learner develops a sense of personal efficacy and assurance that he or she can succeed in academic settings.	4 3 2 1 0
2. Each learner develops a sense that he or she is a valuable and valued part of the learning community.	4 3 2 1 0
3. Each learner understands the learning goals for which he or she is accountable and self-evaluates and self-monitors his or her progress toward achieving them.	4 3 2 1 0
4. Each student experiences the learning environment as personalized and accommodating to his or her interests and learning profiles (i.e., learning style, culture, experiences, gender).	4 3 2 1 0
5. Each student develops cognitively, academically, socially, emotionally, and relationally as a result of his or her interactions with qualified and caring adults.	4 3 2 1 0
Recommendations and Conclusions for Part I:	

Research-Based Organizational Practices for Tenet Four (School Level)	Rating
1. Each student has access to personalized learning and to qualified, caring adults.	4 3 2 1 0
2. The school provides each student access to personalized learning plans, including the ability to design relevant curriculum and course sequencing.	4 3 2 1 0
3. The school uses alternative assessment practices, including the use of portfolios and terminal projects.	4 3 2 1 0
4. The district provides for flexible use of time, enabling high schools to develop alternative approaches to fulfilling the Carnegie Unity (e.g., changing the length of the school year).	4 3 2 1 0
5. The school hires teachers who are highly qualified in pedagogy and subject-area content.	4 3 2 1 0
6. The school provides access to dedicated advisors and mentors for each student.	4 3 2 1 0
7. The school conducts regular school climate surveys of students, staff, and parents.	4 3 2 1 0
8. The school provides opportunities, such as mentoring programs, to ensure that each child has a personal relationship with an adult.	4 3 2 1 0
9. The school implements practices such as morning meetings and advisories to connect students to staff.	4 3 2 1 0

Recommendations and Conclusions for Part II:

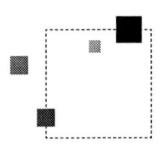

Action Tools Four–Seven: Planning and Implementing Professional Development for Tenet Four

PURPOSE OF THESE TOOLS

This set of action tools will help your team design and implement professional development activities to support your Tenet Four work.

HOW TO USE THE TOOLS

Determine which tools match the needs of the group with which you will be using them. Customize the professional development activities aligned with the needs and goals of the group.

Included with this Tenet Four professional development action tool are the following resources and materials:

1. A Suggested Agenda for Your Tenet Four Professional Development Activities
2. What Is a Personalized Approach to Learning?
3. Investigating Criteria for Ensuring That Each Student Works with Qualified, Caring Adults
4. Implementing and Sustaining Effective Student Advisories, Mentoring Programs, Counseling, and Related Student Support Systems

TIPS AND VARIATIONS

✓ Determine if you wish to develop and implement a Tenet Four–specific professional development program involving initial staff orientation sessions to ensure a common understanding and knowledge base.

✓ If your data analysis process suggests that only some aspects of Tenet Four are underemphasized or display gaps in performance, you may elect to use only those resources and suggestions that directly apply to your priorities.

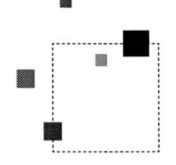

Action Tool Four: A Suggested Agenda for Your Tenet Four Professional Development Activities

PERSONALIZING THE LEARNING PROCESS AND ENSURING THAT ALL LEARNERS WORK WITH QUALIFIED, CARING ADULTS

Objectives: Participants will be able to—

- Explore and understand the key tenets and recommended practices associated with Tenet Four of the Whole Child Compact: (1) personalizing the learning process; and (2) ensuring that all learners work with qualified, caring adults.
- Examine their own work with students and themselves in relationship to promoting Tenet Four priorities.
- Make recommendations for areas in which they and the school might improve in identified Tenet Four priorities.

Suggested Professional Development Activities and Related Resources:

- What Is a Personalized Approach to Learning? (A Professional Development Scenario Brigade!)
- Investigating Criteria for Ensuring That Each Student Works with Qualified, Caring Adults (I'm Talking About the Man—or the Woman—in the Mirror!)
- Implementing and Sustaining Effective Student Advisories, Mentoring Programs, Counseling, and Related Student Support Systems (Dream a Little Dream of Me!)
- Next Steps and Recommendations Based upon Our Activities Today
- Action Planning for Study Groups, Inquiry Teams, and Action Research Projects
- Concluding Discussion: How Does Tenet Four Apply to Our Current School Improvement Planning Process?
- How Can We Address Identified Tenet Four Priority Areas, Gaps, and Omissions via Collaborative Inquiry Processes?

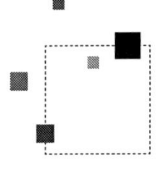

Action Tool Five: What Is a Personalized Approach to Learning? A Professional Development Scenario Brigade!

DIRECTIONS:

1. This activity allows participants to visualize and dramatize their own preferred ways of learning to reinforce the characteristics of a personalized learning environment.
2. Ask each participant to complete the questionnaire in Part I below ("My Preferred Ways of Learning").
3. Then, have them partner with another participant to compare their respective learning profiles.
4. Ask the partner teams to select an area of content knowledge with which they are both familiar. Have them prepare a scenario they will present to the whole group, demonstrating how they would each prefer their learning process be personalized. (If resources and time permit, you may wish to stock the training room with props to dramatize their ideas, such as toys, balloons, music CDs, poster boards, and drawing materials.)
5. At the conclusion of the Scenario Brigade of presentations, ask participants how they might further personalize their own classrooms. As part of their reflection, have them consider the recommendations presented in the checklist in Part II.

PART I: MY PREFERRED WAYS OF LEARNING

Circle the choice in each that best describes your preferred ways of learning.

1. When I learn, I prefer (a) a high degree of light; (b) a medium degree of light; (c) a low degree of light; (d) a combination.
2. When I learn, I prefer (a) a high degree of noise; (b) a medium degree of noise; (c) a low degree of noise; (d) a combination.
3. When I learn, I prefer (a) visual learning tools, particularly print materials; (b) auditory learning tools such as CDs and cassettes; (c) resources that require tactual-kinesthetic interaction, such as math manipulatives; (d) a combination.
4. When I learn, I prefer (a) linear and concrete directions and explanations from the teacher; (b) general directions from the teacher with some degree of allowance for my own decision making; (c) extremely limited directions from the teacher with almost total allowance for my own decision making; (d) a combination.
5. I prefer (a) concrete and practical aspects of curriculum content that are logical and directly relate to my life; (b) creative and emotional-affective aspects of curriculum that allow me to gain insight into how others are feeling and reacting; (c) authentic and real-world projects that allow me to exercise a high degree of independence; (d) a combination.
6. As an assessment tool, I prefer (a) multiple-choice and other forms of selected-response tests and quizzes; (b) creative and artistic projects that allow me to be expressive; (c) very authentic and real-world projects that involve technology and instrumentation; (d) a combination.
7. As a condition for learning, I prefer (a) to have the teacher set the schedule and direct my learning; (b) to set my own schedule with reminders from the teacher; (c) to be open ended in my approach to time and fully in control of deadlines; (d) a combination.
8. I prefer (a) to have the teacher set the evaluation criteria and do all the grading; (b) to have the teacher explain the evaluation criteria and encourage me to apply the criteria to monitoring my own progress; (c) to be free of grades and receive feedback only on my progress in relation to identified standards; (d) a combination.

9. I prefer (a) to learn key facts and concepts without a lot of extraneous material; (b) to learn about cultural and social-relational aspects of the content; (c) to learn the big ideas and themes that unify and connect different aspects of the content.
10. I need (a) to learn what I am supposed to learn and then be finished with it; (b) to revisit big ideas and themes so that I can enrich my growing understanding; (c) to see the immediate uses of what I am learning and forget about the rest; (d) a combination.
11. I enjoy (a) having an impersonal learning environment in which my personality and interests are left alone; (b) having a somewhat personalized learning environment in which my interests are addressed periodically; (c) having a learning environment that is highly personalized and addresses my interests consistently; (d) a combination.
12. I enjoy (a) working alone with a high degree of independence; (b) working with others on a limited basis; (c) working with others as much as possible in a variety of cooperative learning situations; (d) a combination.
13. I need (a) to never have my own background—including my cultural and ethnic identity—brought into the classroom; (b) to have my own background—including my cultural and ethnic identity—addressed sporadically; (c) to have my own background—including my cultural and ethnic identity—acknowledged and addressed frequently; (d) a combination.
14. I believe that (a) the things I am especially interested in should not be a part of my learning in school; (b) the things I am especially interested in should play a small part of my learning in school; (c) the things I am especially interested in should play a large part in my learning at school; (d) a combination.

PART II: SUGGESTIONS FOR PERSONALIZING YOUR CLASSROOM

1. Administer interest surveys to find out about your students and their activities and interests.
2. When feasible, allow students to make suggestions about topics and skills they would like included in a lesson or unit.
3. Periodically allow students to apply what they have learned to authentic and personal situations and settings.
4. Make certain that students' interests and personal backgrounds are highlighted and dignified in class displays, bulletin boards, and other venues.
5. Celebrate student successes and achievements through classroom displays and artifacts.
6. Allow students opportunities to make choices about the performances and products they complete as part of performance tasks and culminating projects.
7. Acknowledge personal accomplishments and milestones for students when they occur.
8. Use town meetings (e.g., weekly 10-minute warm-up discussions) to acknowledge individual accomplishments during the past week.
9. Make certain that every student understands evaluation criteria for which they are responsible via rubrics and checklists—and encourage them to celebrate personal achievements and progress as they learn.
10. Ask students to describe ways that your curriculum and instruction could be personalized for future classes.
11. Find ways to captivate student attention by aligning curriculum content with current interests in the media, news, and so forth.
12. Use humor and visuals to make key points and revisit essential concepts.
13. Employ interesting hook activities at the beginning of lesson segments to stimulate student interest and attention.
14. Vary your approach to teaching, changing focus, content, or strategy every 10 minutes or so.
15. Use technology to focus student attention and captivate student interest.

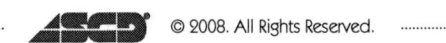

16. Ask students what they have discovered about themselves as they complete important assignments.
17. Have students acknowledge daily a personal growth achievement in your classroom.
18. Use pairs-share and other cooperative learning activities to build camaraderie and group spirit.
19. Periodically use games and tournaments to help students activate their imaginations through nonthreatening competitions.
20. Find opportunities to involve all parts of students' self-system (e.g., cognition, emotions, physical activity, self-image, and self-esteem).

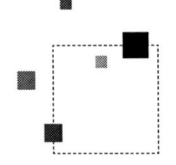

Action Tool Six: Investigating Criteria for Ensuring That Each Student Works with Qualified, Caring Adults: I'm Talking About the Man—or the Woman—in the Mirror!

DIRECTIONS:

1. This professional development activity asks participants to take time to self-reflect and self-evaluate using a checklist for "qualified" and "caring" adults.
2. Use a pairs-share strategy: After participants have completed the checklist questionnaire, ask them to be prepared to share with a partner what they consider their personal strengths and areas that may need tweaking or improvement.
3. You can expand this activity to a pairs-share process in which two pairs combine and share their observations. Ask them to reflect on their areas of commonality and areas of uniqueness.
4. Have the entire training group share insights and implications for ensuring that every student in your school works with caring and qualified adults.

KEY CHARACTERISTICS OF QUALIFIED EDUCATORS

Qualified educators—

- Have met all required state certification requirements.
- Demonstrate an extensive knowledge of core information related to the content they teach.
- Have a deep understanding and appreciation of the content they teach and its significance within the body of world knowledge.
- Make a concerted effort to remain up-to-date on their content area or discipline, ensuring that they learn about and incorporate into their classes any changes or innovations in their field.
- Express a genuine sense of academic enthusiasm to their students, expressing why they love what they are teaching and why they consider it significant for students to learn it.
- Take coursework and participate in professional development designed to keep them well informed and skilled in current educational theory and practice.
- Engage in activities outside of school that enhance their understanding of their content or field of study.
- Work collaboratively with others in significant aspects of school governance and management.
- Understand and apply equitably school and district policies and procedures.
- Are well informed and trained in key facets of child development and learning theory.
- Demonstrate a commitment to reach out to parents, families, and other members of the community served by the school, including sustained commitment to ensuring positive communication with key stakeholders.
- Are well informed about and know how to access health and human services that one or more of their students may need or benefit from.

- Maintain an active and positive role in staff interactions and team building.
- Keep abreast of research-based best practices and use them in their classroom, including innovations in curriculum, instruction, assessment, and classroom management.
- Understand classroom management techniques that can differentiate instruction and assessment to accommodate students' varying readiness levels, interests, and learning profiles.

KEY CHARACTERISTICS OF CARING EDUCATORS

Caring educators—

- Get to know each of their students, including their backgrounds, interests, and learning profiles.
- Demonstrate concern and appreciation for each of their students on a regular basis.
- Strive to integrate personal and positive comments to every student as much as possible.
- Use a range of strategies to communicate affection and support for each student (e.g., greeting them at the door, using their names, making positive comments).
- Keep well informed about how students are progressing—and intervene appropriately and quickly when students demonstrate academic, emotional, or social-relational problems.
- Strive to bring student interests into the content, personalizing activities whenever possible.
- Use a variety of nonverbal affirmations (e.g., eye contact, smiles, gestures, proximity) to reinforce positive relationships with each student.
- Use humor when appropriate.
- Communicate a sense of fairness and objectivity to every student.
- Demonstrate a high degree of personal efficacy and self-restraint, ensuring that they remain objective when handling disturbances or disciplinary problems.

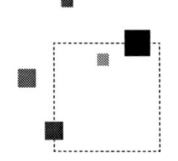

Action Tool Seven: Implementing and Sustaining Effective Student Advisories, Mentoring Programs, Counseling, and Related Student Support Systems—Dream a Little Dream of Me!

DIRECTIONS:

1. Invite participants to dream a little and imagine what a true support system for every student might look like if you had the resources (human and material).
2. Ask them to form "dream teams" responsible for creating and presenting their vision for a comprehensive student support system that fully addresses the needs and developmental requirements of every learner in your school.
3. Use the suggestions presented below for a starting point. Then, use flip-chart paper to present a verbal or nonverbal (e.g., pictograph, graphic organizer, flow chart) representation of the support system you are proposing. As part of your discussion, be prepared to compare your "dream" to the reality of your current school-based support services and programs for students. How closely do they align?
4. After each team has had a chance to present their dream visions, ask the entire group to provide feedback about the implications of this activity for your work with Tenet Four.

STUDENT ADVISORIES

Student advisories can take a variety of forms. Specifically, however, they require that each student be assigned an advisor who has the time to work with them on a regular basis. Ideally, advisors move across grade levels with the student, remaining a firm part of the student's support system. Student advisors should be well trained in identified areas in which the student may require intervention, extra support, tutoring, or intervention via health and human services. The advisor does not have to be one of the student's teachers. In an ideal situation, student advisory meetings are a regular part of the formal school schedule.

COUNSELING SERVICES

Counseling services should be immediately accessible to students to serve a variety of needs. The traditional guidance counselor's role, of course, is most often associated with this element of a support system. However, counseling services should include options for students to access psychological counseling and health services offered either on-site or through agencies and clinics close to the school. An especially important part of effective counseling services is a limitation on counselor-to-student ratios. Part of a true vision for effective and multifaceted counseling services is reducing the number of students assigned to each counselor, greatly improving the potential for providing substantive counseling services.

MENTORING

Mentors encourage the student and establish a genuine and sustained rapport with him or her. Unlike a faculty advisor, a mentor's role should be relatively nonstructured and can include a range of services and support functions. An important part of effective mentoring is for the mentor to understand and establish direct contact with the mentee's family, asking them for support in providing appropriate services. Ideally, every student should have a significant and highly accessible adult to depend on to be a mentor.

ON-SITE HEALTH AND HUMAN SERVICES

Increasingly, multiservice schools are offering health and human services right at the school site. Generally, doing so requires cross-institutional partnerships with health agencies, social service agencies, and other government and private service entities. Typically, this process begins with a health clinic located on campus, but it can be expanded to family services offered on site. An especially important component is expanded availability of psychologists and social workers who can provide immediate intervention and support for students and families in need.

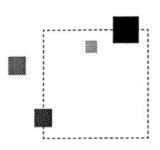

Action Tool Eight: Study Group Articles and Discussion Questions

PURPOSE OF THIS TOOL

This tool provides suggestions for *Educational Leadership* articles in electronic format for use in your Tenet Four study groups. The electronic articles are available for download at www.ascd.org/downloads.

HOW TO USE THIS TOOL

Refer to the study guideline and tools included in the Overview section to support the planning and implementation of your study group.

Study Group Articles and Discussion Questions

Personalizing the Learning Process:

1. **Robert J. Sternberg (2006, September). Recognizing neglected strengths.** *Educational Leadership, 64*(1), 30–35.

    - Sternberg asserts that research is confirming that students in underrepresented minority groups have culturally relevant knowledge and diverse cognitive abilities that often go unnoticed. What are the problems resulting from this practice?
    - How can educators incorporate students' practical knowledge and skills in their efforts to personalize the learning environment?

2. **Mary Hatwood Futrell & Joel Gomez (2008, May). Special topic / How tracking creates a poverty of learning.** *Educational Leadership, 65*(8), 74–78.

    - Why do the authors assert that to close the achievement gap, we must challenge the inequity created by ability grouping?
    - What are the implications of Futrell and Gomez's assertions for personalizing the learning environment?
    - How can you use the ideas presented in this article to support your work with Tenet Four?

3. **Jennifer Carolan & Abigail Guinn (2007, February). Differentiation: Lessons from master teachers.** *Educational Leadership, 64*(5), 44–47.

    - What are the essential characteristics of differentiation as the authors present them?
    - How can educators make use of "personalized scaffolding" to maximize the achievement of each learner?
    - What do the authors mean when they recommend "using flexible means to reach defined ends"? What are the implications of their recommendations for your Whole Child Initiative?

4. **Carol Ann Tomlinson & Jane Jarvis (2006, September). Teaching beyond the book.** *Educational Leadership, 64*(1), 16–21.

    - Why do Tomlinson and Jarvis recommend that educators "stop studying the how-to list and start studying [their] students"?
    - What does it mean to "teach to the strengths in students"?
    - How might the differentiated practices presented in this article contribute to improving the achievement of each student in your school or district?

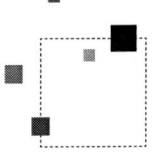

Action Tool Nine: Inquiry Team and Action Research Questions

PURPOSE OF THIS TOOL

This tool will support your planning process for the tenet and also guide implementation and evaluation of what is working.

HOW TO USE THIS TOOL

Determine which questions are aligned with your school community's needs and goals. Use the inquiry and action research tools included in the Overview section to guide your work.

TIPS AND VARIATIONS

✓ Have small groups select three to five different inquiry or action research questions as a focus area. Share plans and actions resulting from discussions, and action research results in ongoing learning community meetings.

Inquiry Team and Action Research Questions

Tenet Four Inquiry Focus Questions

1. To what extent does each learner in our school demonstrate a sense of personal efficacy?
2. How assured do our students appear to be that they can succeed in academic settings? How do we know?
3. What barriers and problems seem to interfere with our students' sense of efficacy?
4. What works against some of our students feeling that they can be successful in school?
5. To what extent does each of our students develop a sense that he or she is a valuable part of our learning community?
6. To what extent does each student understand the learning goals for which he or she is accountable?
7. How do we determine that our students understand what they are learning and why they are learning it?
8. How do we ask students to self-evaluate and monitor their progress toward achieving identified learning goals?
9. To what extent does each student develop a capacity for metacognition and self-regulation?
10. What barriers or omissions contribute to students' lack of metacognitive awareness?
11. To what extent does each student experience the learning environment as personalized?
12. How do we accommodate and address students' interests as part of the teaching-learning process?
13. To what extent do we develop and address student learning profiles, including ways in which the following affect learning: preferred learning styles, culture, experiences, and gender?
14. How well do we support each student's cognitive development?
15. How well do we support each student's academic performance?
16. To what extent do we help each student to develop and grow socially? How formalized is our approach to monitoring students' social growth?
17. How do we help students to grow and develop emotionally? How effective are we in monitoring this growth?
18. To what extent does each student develop positive relationships with others as a result of his or her interactions with qualified and caring adults?
19. To what extent does each student have access to personalized learning?
20. To what extent does each student work with qualified, caring adults?
21. How does the school personalize the learning plan for each student? How effectively do we monitor these plans?
22. To what extent does our school use alternative and balanced assessment practices, including portfolios and exit projects?
23. How have we attempted to balance accountability-based assessments (e.g., standardized tests) with more personalized and student-centered approaches to assessment?
24. To what extent does our district provide for flexible use of time, enabling high schools to develop alternative approaches to fulfilling the Carnegie Unity (e.g., changing the length of the school year)?
25. How does each school ensure that it hires teachers who are highly qualified in instructional design and strategies?
26. How effective is the school in hiring teachers with solid professional understanding of effective pedagogy?
27. To what extent does our school provide access for every student to dedicated advisors and mentors?
28. How often do we conduct school climate surveys of students, staff, and parents? How do we use the data from these surveys?

29. To what extent do mentoring programs and similar services ensure that each child has a sustained personal relationship with one or more caring adults?
30. How does the school make use of practices such as morning meetings and advisories to connect students to staff?

Tenet Four Action Research Questions

1. How will developing and implementing an observation checklist for student efficacy affect our ability to identify and promote behaviors associated with student engagement?
2. How can we identify and emphasize instructional strategies to support each student's sense of personal confidence? How will implementing one or more of these strategies improve the confidence of our students?
3. How can we identify and implement strategies to support students to overcome barriers to academic achievement associated with the effects of socioeconomic conditions?
4. How can we identify and implement strategies to support students to overcome barriers to academic achievement resulting from low self-esteem?
5. How can we identify and implement strategies to support students to overcome barriers to academic achievement resulting from home conditions that may impede learning?
6. How will developing and implementing a schoolwide program of higher-order questioning strategies affect student understanding of academic content?
7. To what extent will our expanded use of in-class reflective assessments (e.g., reflective journals, interviews, think-pair-shares, exit slips) improve students' metacognitive awareness and self-monitoring?
8. How will using rubrics or scoring scales to describe levels of proficiency for each of our major academic learning goals enhance students' understanding of those goals?
9. How will using rubrics or scoring scales to describe levels of proficiency for each of our major academic learning goals enhance students' ability to self-monitor and self-assess?
10. How will implementing in all classrooms research-based strategies to personalize the learning environment affect student achievement and motivation?
11. How will identifying and addressing students' interests as a regular part of the teaching-learning process enhance their academic performance?
12. How will developing and addressing student learning profiles affect academic achievement and student motivation?
13. How can we address individual students' preferred learning styles? How will emphasizing this component of learning affect student performance?
14. To what extent will our use of culture-sensitive curriculum materials affect student performance?
15. How will formalizing our approach to monitoring students' social growth affect achievement and motivation?
16. How will increasing our overt attention to students' social-emotional growth and development support achievement of our performance targets for students?
17. How will expanded emphasis on developing positive student-teacher and peer-peer relationships affect student achievement and motivation?
18. How will formalized approaches to personalizing the learning environment for every student affect their learning process? For example, how might developing and monitoring a personalized learning plan for every student affect student achievement and motivation?

19. How can we achieve consensus about and formalize the characteristics for qualified, caring adults in our building? How will integrating this process into our professional development activities affect school climate and student achievement?
20. How will expanding our emphasis on balancing accountability-based assessments (e.g., standardized tests) with more personalized and student-centered approaches to assessment affect student achievement and motivation?
21. How will developing and implementing an advisory and mentoring program for our students affect their motivation, efficacy, and achievement?
22. How can incorporating annual school climate goals into our school improvement plan enhance organizational productivity and student achievement?

TENET FIVE TOOLS

Preparing Each Student for College, Postgraduation Study, and Work in a Global Environment

INTRODUCTION 181

TITLE OF TOOL

1. Exploring Key Criteria Associated with Tenet Five 183

2. Examining Your School's Current Status—Strategies for Data Collection and Analysis for Tenet Five 187

3. Examining Research-Based Best Practices for Tenet Five. 191

4–7: Planning and Implementing Professional Development for Tenet Five 195

    4. Suggested Agenda for Your Tenet Five Professional Development Activities 196

    5. Meta-Skills and Competencies to Ensure Each Student's Success in the 21st Century 197

    6. Suggestions for Flexible Graduation Requirements— Building Consensus Using an Opinion Line 200

    7. Understanding the 21st Century Workplace 202

8. Study Group Articles and Discussion Questions 205

9. Inquiry Team and Action Research Questions 209

Preparing Each Student for College, Postgraduation Study, and Work in a Global Environment

Introduction

This section will help educators and community members to address two primary goals related to the final tenet of the Whole Child Compact: (1) to ensure that each student is prepared for success in college or further postgraduation study and (2) to ensure that each student is prepared for success in a global environment. In our change-dominated and technology-driven world, these priorities seem especially relevant and crucial for the economic and social prosperity of our students as they confront their future. The preparation provided by schools and communities is a critical component for student success.

Making this fifth tenet a reality involves a combination of complex policy changes, transformation of high schools (and their connection to elementary and middle school feeder patterns), and an increased awareness of the implications of rapidly changing economic conditions and globalization. As stakeholders investigate ways to achieve the vision implicit in this tenet, they may wish to begin with a consideration of the parameters of this challenge as they are presented in recent publications and research studies.

For example, the report *Ready for Tomorrow: Helping All Students Achieve Secondary and Postsecondary Success—A Guide For Governors* (National Governors Association, 2003) makes a series of powerful recommendations in this area. With state governors as their primary audience, the authors of this report address the policy changes needed at the state level to increase attendance and completion of postsecondary education, especially for minority students. Their key recommendations include the following:

- Set a statewide benchmark for postsecondary attainment.
- Create and support an integrated K–16 data system.
- Better align K–12 and higher education expectations and incentives.
- Promote more learning options.
- Focus on low-performing high schools.

According to Kazis, Pennington, and Conklin, as many as 30 percent of entering freshmen—and as many as 60 percent in some large urban districts—leave school without a regular high school diploma. The percentage of high school graduates peaked in 1970 at 77 percent and has not increased since. Those who do graduate from high school are often not prepared for college: one-third of all college freshmen take a remedial class; three-fourths of freshmen in urban community colleges do so. The fastest-growing segments of most states' high school and college-age populations are groups that have the greatest academic disadvantages.

Perhaps most significant, this tenet emphasizes the need for all students to experience an education that promotes their creative self-expression, critical thinking, and capacity for self-regulation and self-monitoring. Lichtenberg, Woock, and Wright (2008), for example, describe organizational contradictions evident in many schools today in *Ready to Innovate: Are Educators and Executives Aligned on the Creative Readiness of the U.S. Workforce?* This report discusses how both school administrators and employers perceive creativity as increasingly important in U.S. workplaces, but do not implement training to develop creative skills:

- Both superintendents and employers find that foremost in demonstrating creativity are the ability to identify new patterns of behavior or new combinations of actions and integration of knowledge across different disciplines. Other responsibilities show a lack of alignment between employers and superintendents.
- Employers say problem identification or articulation best demonstrates creativity, while school superintendents rank it ninth. Superintendents rank problem solving first; employers rank it eighth. These discrepancies bolster the view that while schools teach students how to solve problems put before them, the business sector requires workers who can identify the problems in the first place.

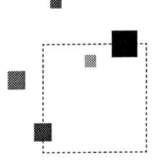

Action Tool One: Exploring Key Criteria Associated with Tenet Five

PURPOSE OF THIS TOOL

Tenet Five is especially challenging in that it requires stakeholders to examine their entire preK–12 educational system and its connections to both postsecondary education and the 21st century world of work. This tool provides a series of recommendations for you to consider using with key stakeholder groups. Its purpose is to offer a range of initial questions for discussion and focus groups to consider and use. These initial sessions can be a part of your Community Conversation process, or they can be used as follow-up data gathering activities related to key elements of Tenet Five. This tool can begin to guide your planning to support the following goals:

- Ensure that each student is prepared for success in college or further study;
- Expand opportunities for the success of each student in other forms of postsecondary education; and
- Prepare each student for success in the 21st century workplace.

HOW TO USE THIS TOOL

Consider the recommendations in this tool as catalysts for your strategic planning for Tenet Five. How might each of the stakeholder groups be involved in providing suggestions and observations about the quality of your current curriculum—especially at the high school level? This tool can also be used to elicit reactions from stakeholders about the quality of graduates in your district as they enter postsecondary education institutions, including colleges, universities, and training schools. Finally, you can use the ideas in this tool to begin or sustain conversations about how you are preparing students for the global environment and workplace of the 21st century.

TIPS AND VARIATIONS

✓ Share a synthesis of your community discussions and focus group sessions on your school Web site or as a published report. It can become a useful and interesting catalyst for dealing with issues of high school reform and improvement of communication and planning among elementary, middle, and high schools that form a feeder pattern.

Exploring Key Criteria Associated with Tenet Five

Directions: Orientation and initial focus group activities for Tenet Five should include a range of options for engaging community stakeholders in start-up discussions and planning. For this tool the facilitator should

- Divide the group into pairs representing varied stakeholders (e.g., business representative and service agency representative). In each pair, identify one person as partner A and one as partner B.
- Give each pair a numbered section below.
- Have pairs stand and face their partner.
- For the first round, partner A discusses pertinent ideas from a selected question and shares for one minute; partner B listens.
- For the second round, partner B discusses pertinent ideas from a selected question and shares for one minute; partner A listens.
- Continue with additional rounds if needed, with partners alternating roles.
- At the end of the discussion, have pairs jot down the three most important points shared and give them to the facilitator.
- The important points can then be used to inform planning for Tenet Five.

1. Parents, Guardians, and Families: Initial outreach sessions and focus group activities can be structured around engaging stakeholders in an open dialogue and forum focused upon the following questions:

    - How successful are we in ensuring that each student succeeds in a college or university setting?
    - How can we expand opportunities for each student to succeed in other forms of postsecondary education?
    - What are your hopes for your student(s) in terms of career pathways and career options?
    - What are the unique challenges of the 21st century workplace? How can we work together to prepare students for success in our global economy?

2. Community Stakeholders: In addition to parents, guardians, and other family members, another key focus for planning sessions for Tenet Five can involve community representatives in a discussion of the same questions. Additional questions might include the following:

    - Based on your own experiences, how successful do you think our high schools are in offering rigorous educational programs and options for each student?
    - What can we do to enhance the success of each student in postsecondary education and career pathways?

3. Businesses and Corporations: Obviously, this fifth tenet is of great concern and interest to representatives of your business community, including major corporations in your area. Specific focus questions involving representatives from this sector include the following:

    - In your opinion, what are the unique characteristics and challenges of the workplace and economy of the 21st century?
    - How successful are our graduates when they enter the workforce?
    - What have you observed about the knowledge, skills, and preparedness of our graduates?

- What suggestions can you make for enhancing each student's education to better prepare our graduates for post-secondary education and the world of work?
- To what extent can we improve our students' workplace competencies, including their work ethic, responsibility, teamwork, and technology competency?

4. Service Agencies: Representatives from various agencies in your community responsible for health and human services can provide a unique and valuable perspective on this fifth tenet and schools' ability to address it. Focus questions for discussions and planning sessions can include the following:

- What are your observations and assessments of our graduates' social, emotional, and relational strengths and needs?
- In your opinion, how successful are our high schools in preparing each student for success in postsecondary educational institutions?
- What are the unique challenges and requirements for ensuring the success of each student in the workplace of the 21st century?
- How might we collaborate to expand each students' access to needed health and human services through cross-institutional collaborations and partnerships?

5. College, University, and Other Postsecondary Education Institutions: One of the most important cross-institutional partnerships in support of this fifth tenet is, of course, postsecondary institutional representatives. Their professional vantage point gives them unique insights into the preparedness of each graduate for success in their respective schools. Following are suggested questions for discussions and planning sessions with these stakeholders:

- How successful are our graduates when they attend your particular institution?
- Are there general patterns you can identify?
- Are there additional insights you can share about subgroups of our graduates? For example, how successful are students from various racial, ethnic, gender, and socioeconomic groups when they attend your school?
- What recommendations can you give us for enhancing the rigor and excellence of our curriculum and educational programs?
- How can we extend our collaboration and partnership to prepare each graduate for postsecondary education and the world of work?

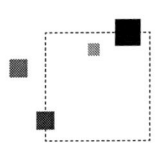

Action Tool Two: Examining Your School's Current Status—Strategies for Data Collection and Analysis for Tenet Five

PURPOSE OF THIS TOOL

This tool can be used as an informal template for considering ways in which you can establish baseline data about the quality of student preparation for postsecondary education and the world of work.

HOW TO USE THIS TOOL

You may wish to use this tool in anticipation of administering a more formal survey, with your Whole Child planning team discussing their reactions to this tool. In which areas does there seem to be major agreement? In which areas does there seem to be a lack of consensus? Consider also the suggestions for preliminary data gathering and analysis—and ways these processes can complement your strategic and school improvement planning activities.

TIPS AND VARIATIONS

- ✓ Keep your initial data-gathering and analysis information as part of your record for your Whole Child planning process. Such field data can be useful in preserving an ongoing portrait of your school or district in transition.
- ✓ Periodically revisit the same process, comparing ongoing data patterns and recommendations. To what extent does this process reveal improvements in identified areas? To what extent do gaps in achievement or organizational productivity seem to persist?

Examining Your School's Current Status—Strategies for Data Collection and Analysis for Tenet Five

Part I: Determining Current Student Achievement Levels

Directions:
1. Ask representative stakeholders (e.g., teachers, administrators, parents, family members, community members, representatives of local businesses) to use the following rating scale to assess each of the following student outcomes associated with Whole Child Tenet Five: 4 = Highly evident for all students; 3 = Evident for a majority of students; 2 = Evident for some but not a majority of students; 1 = Evident for few students; 0 = Not evident.
2. Collect this initial data and analyze significant patterns and trends.
3. Use the questions at the end of this section to initiate your action plan for addressing identified priorities.

Student Outcomes	Rating
1. The student sets and achieves life goals that include education beyond high school.	4 3 2 1 0
2. The student successfully completes all state-mandated graduation requirements.	4 3 2 1 0
3. The student displays mastery of skills necessary to enter and succeed in postsecondary educational settings (e.g., academic, social, civic, technological, vocational).	4 3 2 1 0
4. The student understands the characteristics of the global environment, including its diversity and interconnectedness.	4 3 2 1 0
5. The student demonstrates emotional intelligence, including the capacity to work effectively with others in one-on-one and team situations.	4 3 2 1 0
6. The student displays meta-skills and habits of mind necessary for success in a change-dominated, technology-driven, and economically interdependent world (e.g., time management, self-regulation, communication, problem solving, decision making, and social interaction).	4 3 2 1 0
7. The student develops the technological competencies to succeed in a 21st century environment, including technical proficiencies, understanding of technology, media literacy, and willingness to adapt to technological change.	4 3 2 1 0

Suggested Follow-Up Planning Questions

Based on your initial results, address the following questions:
- What have we concluded to be major student achievement gaps?
- What data can we collect to triangulate our initial conclusions?
- As we examine the suggested priorities presented below, how might we begin to address identified gaps and needs?
- How will we include our suggestions in our school improvement plan?

Action Tool Two: Examining Your School's Current Status—
Strategies for Data Collection and Analysis for Tenet Five

Part II: Determining Current Levels of Organizational Practice

Directions:
1. Ask representative stakeholders (e.g., teachers, administrators, parents, family members, community members, representatives of local businesses) to use the following rating scale to assess the present level of organizational practice for each element below associated with Whole Child Tenet Five: 4 = Highly evident; 3 = Evident; 2 = Needs more emphasis; 1 = Needs much more emphasis; 0 = Not evident and needs immediate emphasis.
2. Collect these initial data and analyze significant patterns and trends.
3. Use the questions at the end of this section to initiate your action plan for addressing identified priorities.

Organizational Practice	Rating
1. Cross-institutional partnerships (e.g., mentorships, school-university collaborations, concurrent enrollment options) expand students' access to postsecondary and career development opportunities.	4 3 2 1 0
2. Schools maintain flexible graduation requirements.	4 3 2 1 0
3. Graduation requirements are aligned with state or provincial laws, policies, and regulations.	4 3 2 1 0
4. Assessment of students' progress ensures that all learners receive appropriate interventions and support resources to maximize their achievement.	4 3 2 1 0
5. A range of curriculum opportunities exists for all students to ensure that they can accelerate and personalize their education, including such programs as advanced placement, International Baccalaureate, work/study, internships/externships, and college credit options.	4 3 2 1 0
6. The school provides opportunities for community-based apprenticeships, internships, and projects.	4 3 2 1 0
7. Enrichment experiences complement extracurricular activities and programs to ensure that all students have a range of options for enhancing their academic background knowledge.	4 3 2 1 0
8. The school monitors each student's development of competencies necessary for a 21st century environment, including technical proficiencies, understanding of technology, media literacy, and willingness to adapt to technological change.	4 3 2 1 0

Suggested Follow-Up Action Planning Questions

Based on your initial results, address the following questions:
- What have we concluded to be major organizational omissions or gaps?
- What data can we collect to triangulate our initial conclusions?
- As we examine these issues, how might we begin to address identified gaps and needs?
- How will we include our suggestions in our school improvement plan?
- Who are key players? How will we involve the community and students?
- What are the implications of these changes for service-learning projects?

Tenet Five

© 2008. All Rights Reserved.

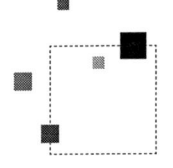

Action Tool Three: Examining Research-Based Best Practices for Tenet Five

PURPOSE OF THIS TOOL

This tool provides a detailed overview of current recommendations in the major components of Tenet Five, including exit skills, curriculum reform, program enhancements, and ideas for better equipping students for postsecondary education and the world of work.

HOW TO USE THIS TOOL

This tool can be used to (1) initiate Community Conversations related to Tenet Five, (2) promote staff discussions of how successfully a school is preparing each student for college and postgraduation study, (3) facilitate stakeholder discussions about how successfully a school is preparing each student for work in a global environment, and (4) inform professional development plans in support of Tenet Five.

TIPS AND VARIATIONS

- ✓ Consider how trends and data patterns reflect stakeholder perception about your K–12 program, post-secondary opportunities, and workplace preparation.
- ✓ Incorporate ideas and recommendations from stakeholder reactions to this tool into your school improvement plan.
- ✓ Examine ways community outreach and cross-institutional partnerships can assist you in addressing key issues and priorities that emerge from using this tool.

Examining Research-Based Best Practices for Tenet Five

Directions: Select a facilitator to lead the following activity:

- The facilitator creates and posts a chart for "Skills and Competencies for the 21st Century" and a chart for "Research-Based Organizational Practices."
- Next to each posted chart is a blank piece of chart paper.
- Individuals read the numbered statements on each chart and record personal reflections answering the question: What strategies, practices, and policies do we need to implement to support all students in these areas?
- The facilitator divides the group in half.
- Each group lines up in front of a designated chart.
- The first person in each group writes their suggestion, passes the pen to the person behind them, then takes a seat.
- The process continues until all have either written a suggestion or placed a check mark to agree with a suggestion.
- Depending on the amount of time and input needed from each group, the facilitator can repeat the process by having groups switch charts.
- The facilitator can lead a debriefing discussion focused on the suggestions with the most check marks to inform the planning and solution development process for Tenet Five.

Skills and Competencies for the 21st Century
1. Critical thinking and reasoning skills (e.g., analysis; synthesis; evaluation; ability to discern errors in logic; and the capacity to present and defend claims, assertions, and arguments)
2. Problem-solving competencies (i.e., the ability to identify problems and related barriers, discern alternative approaches to solving identified problems, determine the most viable approach, and execute an action plan to solve them)
3. Decision making (i.e., the ability to determine goals, generate criteria for evaluating alternative approaches, and use a rational approach to making final decisions)
4. Communication skills (e.g., the ability to express oneself to an identified audience using a variety of modalities, including writing, speaking, and multimedia)
5. Mathematical problem-solving and data-analysis competencies (i.e., the capacity to apply mathematical algorithms and processes to the collection and analysis of data and the ability to use essential statistical operations to discern patterns and draw inferences)
6. Interpersonal competencies (e.g., active listening, conflict resolution, empathy, capacity to operate effectively as part of a team)
7. Ethical citizenship (i.e., the ability to function successfully as a citizen, including understanding such concepts as rights and responsibilities)
8. Multicultural awareness and empathy (i.e., a recognition of the diversity of the human experience and understanding of a range of multicultural elements such as race, ethnicity, religion, region, socioeconomic differences, and gender)
9. Career awareness and preparation (e.g., goal setting, understanding the requirements for identified career pathways, self-monitoring to ensure successful preparation for desired career paths)
10. Workplace competencies (i.e., universal skills required for any professional setting, including time management, professional communication, and human interaction skills)
11. Technology proficiency (i.e., the ability to use technology for communication, information accessing, presentations, and analysis)

Research-Based Organizational Practices (School Level)
1. Emphasize "global competencies" such as foreign language skills and civic values. Schools can do this by • Introducing an international studies requirement for graduation • Creating elementary school immersion programs • Developing international schools-within-schools • Teaching crucial language skills to prepare for the global economy • Redesigning urban secondary schools with an international focus • Using student-faculty exchanges to promote curriculum change • Using a K–12 foreign language sequence to promote excellence. (*Educational Leadership* 2007, April)
2. Help students to develop cognitive skills such as interpretation, instrumentation, interaction, and inner direction.
3. Ensure that high expectations and frequent feedback are integrated into classroom practices, including rigorous academic studies that encourage all students to apply academic content and skills to real-world problems.
4. Provide intellectually challenging career and technical studies programs and work-based learning planned collaboratively by educators, employers, and students.
5. Emphasize professional collaboration in which teachers work together in interdisciplinary teams to integrate reading, writing, and speaking into all parts of the curriculum and to integrate mathematics into the science and career and technical curricula.
6. Ensure that each student is actively engaged in assignments and learning activities involving research-based instructional strategies and technology.
7. Provide a guidance and advisement system that gives each student the same mentor throughout high school and ensures the student's completion of an accelerated program of study with an academic or career/technical concentration.
8. Develop and sustain a structured system of extra help, coaching, tutorials, and counseling to address each student's unique strengths and needs.
9. Create a culture of continuous improvement based on student assessment and program evaluation data.

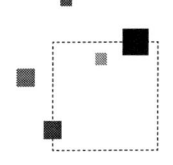

Action Tools Four–Seven: Planning and Implementing Professional Development for Tenet Five

PURPOSE OF THESE TOOLS

This set of action tools will help your team design and implement professional development activities to support your Tenet Five work.

HOW TO USE THESE TOOLS

Determine which tools match the needs of the group with which you will be using them. Customize the professional development activities aligned with the needs and goals of the group.

TIPS AND VARIATIONS

- ✓ Whole Child strategic planning teams may wish to use the elements in this section as a framing tool for exploring all other tenets.
- ✓ If your data analysis process suggests that only some aspects of Tenet Five are underemphasized or display gaps in performance, you may elect to use only those tools that directly apply to your most immediate Tenet Five priorities.

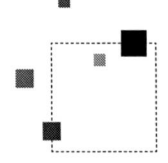

Action Tool Four: Suggested Agenda for Your Tenet Five Professional Development Activities

Objectives: Participants will be able to—

- Explore and understand the key principles and recommended practices associated with Tenet Five of the Whole Child Compact: (1) preparing every student for postsecondary education, (2) equipping every learner with 21st century competencies, and (3) ensuring that every student is equipped for success in the world of work.
- Examine their own work with students and themselves in relationship to promoting Tenet Five priorities.
- Make recommendations for areas in which they and the school might improve in identified Tenet Five priorities.

Suggested Professional Development Activities

- Exploring Key Elements of a 21st Century Curriculum
- Meta-Skills and Competencies to Ensure Each Student's Success in the 21st Century
- Investigating Flexible Graduation Requirements
- Understanding the 21st Century Workplace
- Next Steps and Recommendations Based on Our Activities Today
- Action Planning for Study Groups, Inquiry Teams, and Action Research Projects
- Concluding Discussion: How Does Tenet Five Apply to Our Current School Improvement Planning Process?
- How Can We Address Identified Tenet Five Priority Areas, Gaps, and Omissions via Collaborative Inquiry Processes?

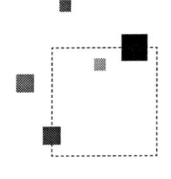

Action Tool Five: Meta-Skills and Competencies to Ensure Each Student's Success in the 21st Century: A Professional Development JIGSAW Activity

DIRECTIONS:

1. Indicate to participants that they will become experts on what well-known educators, community leaders, and corporate heads are saying today about the skills and competencies high school graduates should bring with them into post-secondary education and the world of work.
2. Have participants form five review groups of three to five people. Each group will be given one of the cards below to reflect on and debate. Ask them to consider such questions as the following:
   - What are the main ideas on our card?
   - To what extent do we agree with what the card says?
   - What are the implications of the ideas presented on our card for our students, particularly our graduates?
   - To what extent are we addressing the ideas and issues presented on our card?
   - To what extent are improvements needed?
3. At the conclusion of the breakout group discussions, teams will reconfigure so that each new group has a representative from each of the original five review groups. In the newly assembled groups, participants will summarize their respective cards and the conclusions of their review group. Ideally, this activity should take 20 to 30 minutes.
4. If time permits, participants should reassemble in whole-group format to share insights and observations, especially how these ideas relate to their school's work with Tenet Five.

CARD ONE

Schools hold themselves accountable for ensuring that each student entrusted to them has the academic and cultural tools needed to succeed—and to create a lifelong passion for learning. These schools have a clear understanding of what their students should know and be able to do, and an even clearer understanding of how children and adolescents learn. No two students are the same, and the most successful schools and districts reflect this fact. No graduate's education is complete without opportunities to develop applied skills necessary for the workplace. Often these skills—such as teamwork, critical thinking, and communication—are essential parts of athletics, music, and community-based projects—areas that are fighting for time in the school schedule. Students need time in the arts, civics, and traditional academics to hone these skills within both the school and the community. A 2006 survey of human resources professionals found that high school graduates lacked competence in these essential skills (Conference Board et al., 2006).

CARD TWO

A study by the Conference Board and others (2006) found the following:

- More than half (58 percent) of responding employers say critical thinking and problem-solving skills are "very important" for incoming high school graduates' successful job performance.
- Nearly three-quarters of respondents (70 percent) rated recently hired high school graduates as deficient in critical thinking.
- Twenty-eight percent of employers project that their companies will reduce hiring of new entrants with only a high school diploma over the next five years, while 49.5 percent said they would hire more two-year college graduates.
- Almost 60 percent said their hires of four-year college graduates would increase.

CARD THREE

Every student should engage in a broad spectrum of activities in and out of the classroom. Districts and communities work together to prepare young people for success in higher education and employment by providing meaningful learning experiences and opportunities to demonstrate achievement. The Whole Child Initiative aligns with the commitment to ensuring the success of each learner. At the same time, however, it connects very powerfully to the economic survival and prosperity of nations coexisting within the global economy of the 21st century.

CARD FOUR

Key skills identified by the Partnership for 21st Century Skills include the following:

- Information and media literacy skills
- Communication skills
- Learning and innovation skills, including creativity and innovation, critical thinking, and problem solving
- Communication and collaboration
- Life and career skills, including flexibility and adaptability, initiative and self-direction, social and cross-cultural skills, productivity and accountability, leadership and responsibility
- Global awareness
- Financial, economic, business, and entrepreneurial literacy
- Civic literacy
- Health literacy

Action Tool Five: Meta-Skills and Competencies to Ensure
Each Student's Success in the 21st Century

CARD FIVE

A recent 21st century skills collaborative partnership of four participating organizations jointly surveyed more than 400 employers across the United States to identify the skills recently hired graduates from high school, two-year colleges or technical schools, and four-year colleges needed to succeed in the workplace. Respondents were asked to project changes in necessary skills over the next five years. The findings reflect anticipated changes in the economy in the near future:

- Sixty-three percent of employers say a foreign language is the most important basic skill students will need.
- Critical thinking and creativity/innovation, two key drivers of a knowledge economy, are expected to increase substantially in importance (77.8 percent for critical thinking and 73.6 percent for creativity/innovation).
- More than three-quarters of respondents (76.1 percent) report that the knowledge and skills necessary to make appropriate choices concerning health and wellness is the number one area in which future needs should be met through education, reflecting the growing rise of health care costs.
- The rate of increase in hiring will be greater for two- and four-year-college graduates than high school graduates, making it imperative for young people to seek higher education (27.7 percent of employers project an increase in four-year-college hires, 49.5 percent project an increase in two-year-college hires).

(The Conference Board, Partnership for 21st Century Skills, Corporate Voices for Working Families and Society for Human Resource Management, accessed at http://www.conference-board.org/pdf_free/BED-06-Workforce.pdf on May 19, 2008)

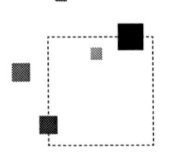

Action Tool Six: Suggestions for Flexible Graduation Requirements—Building Consensus Using an Opinion Line

DIRECTIONS:

1. Encourage staff and other stakeholders to discuss and debate various recommendations for flexible graduation requirements by using the opinion lines included with this activity.
2. Initially, ask each participant to identify where he or she is on the "Opinion Line" in reaction to each of the statements presented.
3. Then three or four participants team up. Ask them to try to achieve consensus on areas of major disagreement and to record areas where they cannot agree.
4. At the conclusion of this exercise, participants can reassemble and the training facilitator can facilitate a consensus-building discussion: Where are we? On what do we seem to agree? On what do we seem to disagree? Where should we go from here?

IDEAS FOR FLEXIBLE GRADUATION REQUIREMENTS

1. Although graduation requirements should be aligned with state or provincial laws, policies, and regulations, school districts should find purposeful ways to accommodate individual students' unique needs, strengths, and talents.

Strongly Disagree	Disagree	No Opinion	Agree	Strongly Agree

   Ideas and Reflections:

2. Assessment results should be used flexibly to monitor students' progress, ensuring that all learners receive appropriate interventions and support services to maximize their achievement toward graduation.

Strongly Disagree	Disagree	No Opinion	Agree	Strongly Agree

   Ideas and Reflections:

3. A range of curriculum and program opportunities should exist for all students to ensure that they can accelerate and personalize their education to ensure their success for postsecondary studies and career pathways.

| Strongly Disagree | Disagree | No Opinion | Agree | Strongly Agree |

Ideas and Reflections:

4. The high school should offer a wide range of acceleration and individual enhancement programs and services, including advanced placement, International Baccalaureate, work study, internships, externships, and concurrent enrollment college credit options.

| Strongly Disagree | Disagree | No Opinion | Agree | Strongly Agree |

Ideas and Reflections:

5. The district should allow seniors to receive high school credit for concurrent enrollment courses taken in local colleges or universities.

| Strongly Disagree | Disagree | No Opinion | Agree | Strongly Agree |

Ideas and Reflections:

6. Cross-institutional partnerships (e.g., mentorships, school-university collaborations, concurrent enrollment options) should be available to every student to expand his or her access to postsecondary education and career development opportunities.

| Strongly Disagree | Disagree | No Opinion | Agree | Strongly Agree |

Ideas and Reflections:

Tenet Five

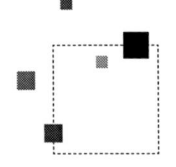

Action Tool Seven: Understanding the 21st Century Workplace—A Professional Development Broadway Production!

DIRECTIONS:

1. This is a chance for participants to put on a show! As they explore the characteristics of the workplace of the 21st century, ask them to form miniature theater troupes of between 3 to 5 participants.
2. Each troupe should imagine that they are graduates of their own school or system. Each graduate has been in the 21st century workplace for more than a decade now.
3. Each troupe will be responsible for creating a 5–10-minute dramatization or performance in which they share with audience members what it has been like for them in the change-dominated, technology-driven workplace of the 21st century.
4. The performance should emphasize three key elements: (a) What is work like for you now and over the last 10 years? (b) How well did your high school prepare you for success? (c) What do you wish had been different about the way you were prepared for the world of work—and for postsecondary education?

READY FOR YOUR PERFORMANCE?

Some Key Issues To Consider As You Prepare For Your Scene!

- Today's graduates are expected to experience between five and seven major career changes during the course of their working lifetimes.
- A single career with a single company or organization will become increasingly archaic as both a concept and a reality.
- The knowledge base we can access is doubling every two to three years as a result of the Internet and related forms of electronic communication.
- Industrial jobs are increasingly being replaced by a global need for information workers.
- Increasingly, major corporations and businesses are advocating cross-functional teaming and constantly changing role requirements, rather than clearly delineated job descriptions.
- Technology and technological innovation dominate the contemporary workplace.
- We exist in an increasingly interdependent economy characterized by many paradoxical elements, including regional competition for scarce resources, growing regional and cross-regional competitiveness, and the rising dominance of the Asian and Pacific Rim countries, particularly India and China.
- American universities now produce more sports management majors than they do mathematicians and engineers.
- Key skills identified by the Partnership for 21st Century Skills include the following "nonnegotiable" workplace competencies:
  - Information and media literacy skills
  - Communication skills
  - Collaboration skills
  - Learning and innovation skills, including creativity and innovation, critical thinking, and problem solving
  - Life and career skills, including flexibility and adaptability, initiative and self-direction, social and cross-cultural skills, productivity and accountability, leadership and responsibility
  - Global awareness
  - Financial, economic, business, and entrepreneurial literacy
  - Civic literacy
  - Health literacy
- People are more often terminated from a position or career because of a lack of emotional intelligence and interpersonal skills than a lack of technical competency.

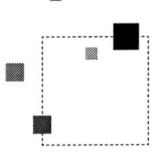

Action Tool Eight: Study Group Articles and Discussion Questions

PURPOSE OF THIS TOOL

This tool provides suggestions for *Educational Leadership* articles in electronic format for use with your Tenet Five study groups. The electronic articles are available for download at www.ascd.org/downloads.

HOW TO USE THIS TOOL

Refer to the study group guidelines and tools included in the Overview section to support the planning and implementation of your study group.

Study Group Articles and Discussion Questions

Transforming the High School

1. Marc Tucker (2007, April). Charting a new course for schools. *Educational Leadership, 64*(7), 48–52.

   - Why does Tucker contend that the United States no longer has the best-educated workforce in the world?
   - What are the recommendations presented in the report, *Tough Choices or Tough Times?* To what extent do you agree with these recommendations?
   - What are the implications of this article for your work in preparing students for postsecondary education and the 21st century workplace?

2. Bob Wise (2008, May). High schools at the tipping point. *Educational Leadership, 65*(8), 8–13.

   - To what extent do you agree with Wise that the U.S. high school is "broken"? What are his arguments for this assertion?
   - What are the implications of the conditions described by Wise for high schools in your area?
   - To what extent do high schools need to be restructured to ensure national competitiveness in a global marketplace?

3. Anthony Jackson (2008, May). High schools in the global age. *Educational Leadership, 65*(8), 58–62.

   - Jackson describes the characteristics of International Studies Schools. What are the common structural elements in these schools?
   - To what extent do these elements offer suggestions for reorganizing and restructuring high schools in your district?
   - How do the global knowledge and skills identified by Jackson align with your expectations for the competencies graduates should exhibit as they enter postsecondary education and the workplace?

4. John D. Forbes & Catherine Richelieu Saunders (2008, May). How we reinvented the high school experience. *Educational Leadership, 65*(8), 42–46.

   - Forbes and Saunders describe a process of "just starting over." To what extent do their assertions and recommendations align with your vision for high school reform?
   - How do high schools in your district currently address the competencies identified in this article: cognition, academics, real-world connections, and personalization?
   - To what extent can the "lessons learned" presented by the authors be used to guide your work with this fifth tenet of the Whole Child Initiative?

Preparing Each Student for Postsecondary Education

1. David T. Conley (2008, May). The challenge of college readiness. *Educational Leadership, 65*(8), 23–29.

   - What are the challenges of getting students ready for college described by Conley? To what extent do you agree that these are universal imperatives?
   - How can your community collaborate on aligning high school curriculum and instruction with college expectations?
   - To what extent are the suggested strategies and processes presented in this article useful in your Whole Child Initiative, particularly Tenet Five?

2. **Grant Wiggins & Jay McTighe (2008, May). Put understanding first.** *Educational Leadership, 65*(8), 36–41.

   - Why do Wiggins and McTighe contend that the long-term goals of schooling should be meaning making and transfer of learning?
   - To what extent do schools in your district reflect the suggested sequence for teaching and learning presented in this article?

3. **Gene Bottoms (2007, April). Treat all Students like the 'Best' students.** *Educational Leadership, 64*(7), 30–37.

   - What are the key elements of the High Schools That Work model?
   - What does it mean to treat all students like the "best" students? To what extent is this practice operational in your school or district?
   - What would your high school look like if the suggestions in this article were fully implemented there?

Emphasizing the Arts, Science, Social Studies, and World Languages for Each Student

1. **Thomas R. Feller Jr., Brian Gibbs-Griffith, Linda D'Acquisto, Claudia Khourey-Bowers, & Cynthia B. Croley (2007, May). Teaching content through the arts.** *Educational Leadership, 64*(8), 48–52.

   - What role do the arts currently play in your school or district?
   - Based on this article's recommendations, how would you assess the level to which the arts are an essential part of your curriculum?
   - What do the authors mean when they say "teaching content through the arts"?
   - How can the strategies and suggestions presented by the authors of this article be incorporated into your Whole Child Initiative?

2. **Thomas M. Irvin (2007, May). Nature lessons.** *Educational Leadership, 64*(8), 54–56.

   - This article is an excellent resource for helping staff to explore the concept of "authentic learning." How does Irvin define and explain this term in his article?
   - What are the article's implications for your work with ensuring that each student is successful in science specifically and learning in general?

Preparing Each Student for the Global Economy and Environment of the 21st Century

1. **Ellen McCarthy, Sandra R. Schecter, John Ippolito, Karine Rashkovsky, Valentine Hart, Louis Cuglietto, Robert Burke, & Steven Ocasio (2007, March). Schools in transition.** *Educational Leadership, 64*(6), 68–73.

   - What do the authors suggest about the impact of student population changes?
   - How do population shifts affect a school's commitment to the Whole Child Initiative?
   - How could design features from the programs and practices presented here be incorporated into your school or district's work with the Whole Child Initiative?

2. **Vivien Stewart (2007, April). Becoming citizens of the world.** *Educational Leadership, 64*(7), 8–14.

   - The author suggests, "The future is here. It's multiethnic, multicultural, and multilingual." How does she answer her own question, "But are students ready for it?"
   - What is global competence? To what extent is this concept emphasized in your school or district?
   - How might you use Stewart's suggestions for "what schools can do" as part of your Whole Child Initiative?

3. **Marcelo M. Suarez-Orozco & Carolyn Sattin (2007, April). Wanted: Global citizens.** *Educational Leadership, 64*(7), 58–62.

   - The authors of this article present a series of recommendations for helping young people to become culturally sophisticated and prepared to work in an international environment. How would you synthesize their major suggestions?
   - To what extent do the students in your school or district reflect the characteristics advocated by the authors?
   - How could you use their suggestions as part of your Whole Child Initiative?

4. **Joe DiMartino & Andrea Castaneda (2007, April). Assessing applied skills.** *Educational Leadership, 64*(7), 38–42.

   - Why do the authors suggest that such practices as the Carnegie unit and awarding course credit for seat time are working against efforts to teach and test 21st century workforce skills?
   - What is the process the authors present for organizing curriculum around applied skills?
   - How might you use their recommendations as part of your work with the Whole Child Initiative?

5. **Richard Rothstein, Tamara Wilder, & Rebecca Jacobsen (2007, May). Balance in the balance.** *Educational Leadership, 64*(8), 8–14.

   - Why do the authors assert that accountability systems in schools should focus on more than basic skills?
   - According to these authors, what school practices and programs are necessary to produce the outcomes needed for success in work and life?
   - Which of the life skills and competencies presented by the authors might become a part of your Whole Child planning process?

Promoting Equity and Excellence in 21st Century Schools

1. **Linda Darling-Hammond & Diane Friedlaender (2008, May). Creating excellent and equitable schools.** *Educational Leadership, 65*(8), 14–21.

   - How would you describe the authors' vision for "high schools for equity"?
   - What role does each of the following play in your current school or district: personalization, rigorous and relevant instruction, and professional learning and collaboration?
   - How might you use the authors' recommendations for policy changes (e.g., organization and governance, human capital, curriculum and assessment, funding) as part of your Whole Child work?

2. **Janet Quint (2008, May). Lessons from leading models.** *Educational Leadership, 65*(8), 64–68.

   - The author of this article presents a series of "snapshots" of successful reform models. What do these models all share in terms of their commitment to the Whole Child Initiative?
   - Which programs and practices presented here might become a part of your action planning for the Whole Child Initiative?

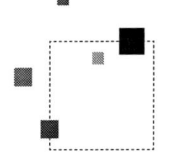

Action Tool Nine: Inquiry Team and Action Research Questions

PURPOSE OF THIS TOOL

This tool will support your planning process for the tenet and also guide implementation and evaluation of what is working.

HOW TO USE THIS TOOL

Determine which questions are aligned with your school community's needs and goals. Use the inquiry and action research tools included in the Overview section to guide your work.

TIPS AND VARIATIONS

✓ Have small groups elect three to five different inquiry or action research questions as a focus area. Share plans and actions resulting from discussions and action research results in ongoing learning community meetings.

Inquiry Team and Action Research Questions

Tenet Five Inquiry Team Focus Questions

1. What is the status of our current efforts to prepare students for postsecondary education? What are our strengths? What are our gaps or weaknesses in this area?
2. To what extent are we in agreement about the 21st century skills and competencies each of our students should master before graduation?
3. What can we do to ensure that we promote students' development of 21st century workplace competencies?
4. How well do we assess and monitor our students' mastery of skills and competencies necessary for success in the world of the 21st century? What are specific ways we might expand and enhance our efforts in this area?
5. How successful are high schools in our region or district? To what extent are they addressing the strengths and needs of each student? How do we know?
6. How successful are we in our current efforts to prepare minority and low-income high school students for postsecondary education and the 21st century workplace? What data sources can we use to answer this question?
7. To what extent would cross-institutional partnerships with local colleges and universities help us to prepare our students for postsecondary education?
8. What is the impact or value added of cross-institutional partnerships with local postsecondary institutions?
9. To what extent do we keep informed and up-to-date about changing college entrance requirements?
10. How do we monitor the achievement of our students when they enter postsecondary settings? To what extent do we modify programs and practices to accommodate changing conditions and needs?
11. What kinds of early warning systems are in place to help minimize high school dropouts? How effective have we been in this area?
12. What programs and practices could we institute to help identify and alleviate emergent problems associated with students' academic, social-emotional, and self-esteem issues?
13. To what extent do our students understand the curriculum they are studying? How do we know?
14. How successful is each of our students in constructing meaning and transferring their learning independently? How do we assess them in this area?
15. How can we blend career and college preparation as part of our high school design?
16. What is the status of the visual and performing arts in our schools, particularly our elementary and middle schools? To what extent can we enhance our efforts in this area?
17. How would we assess the quality of science instruction and learning in our building(s)? How might we improve in this area?
18. How successfully does each of our students gain proficiency and mastery of at least one world language beyond English?
19. How successful are we in dealing with population and demographic shifts in our building(s)? What can we do to improve in areas where we have identified gaps or problems?
20. What does it mean to prepare our students to be citizens of the world? How successful are we in helping them to achieve this goal?
21. To what extent have we integrated technology use and competency into all facets of our curriculum?
22. How effectively do we monitor our students' progress in following chosen career pathways?

23. What can we do to improve our students' ability to succeed in a change-dominated and technology-driven world of work?
24. What are the implications of the global environment and change processes in the modern workplace for each of our students? To what extent are we addressing these issues in students' education?
25. How can we enhance our partnerships and collaboration with government, civic, and business/corporate agencies and organizations to enhance the success of each student in the global environment of the 21st century?
26. To what extent can we enhance and improve our prekindergarten through high school career pathway programs and offerings?

Action Research Questions for Tenet Five
1. How will expanding our emphasis on students' self-monitoring and self-regulation enhance their academic achievement?
2. What is the impact of ensuring that students understand the performance goals and evaluation criteria for which they are accountable?
3. To what extent will holding each student responsible for the same rigorous academic standards enhance individual and aggregate student achievement?
4. How can we hold all students accountable for the same rigorous academic standards while differentiating instruction to accommodate individual readiness levels, interests, and learning profiles?
5. How will building stakeholder consensus about the 21st century competencies that each student should master contribute to student performance in postsecondary education and the world of work?
6. What technology competencies will contribute to student success in postsecondary education and various career pathways? How can we ensure that each student gains proficiency in each competency?
7. What are the entry-level competencies necessary for success in the 21st century workplace? How can we redesign our curriculum, assessment, and instructional systems to promote each student's success in these competencies?
8. What will be the effect of using authentic culminating projects as benchmark assessments to monitor students' progress toward graduation?
9. How will using authentic, real-world design principles in all classrooms affect students' sense of engagement, purpose, and achievement?
10. How will expanding our emphasis on the visual and performing arts impact students' academic achievement, motivation, and engagement?
11. To what extent are we preparing our students to become global citizens? How will modifying existing programs and practices to achieve this goal impact student performance?
12. What are the correlations between increased foreign language requirements and competencies and preparation of students for postsecondary education and the world of work?
13. What impact will service learning projects have on students' understanding of ethical citizenship and their responsibilities as a member of the community?
14. How can we modify social studies programs and curricula to increase each student's understanding of the diversity and multicultural complexity of the world today?
15. How can we enhance our monitoring of students' progress in relation to identified curriculum standards? How will enhancements and modifications in this area contribute to student achievement?

16. How will accelerating and personalizing high school students' education impact their preparation for college, other postsecondary education, and career pathways (e.g., through such programs as advanced placement, International Baccalaureate, work study, internships, college-credit options)?
17. What impact will cross-institutional partnerships (e.g., mentorships, school-university collaborations, concurrent enrollment programs) have on students' academic and career development?

PUTTING IT ALL TOGETHER

The Whole Child Initiative as a Holistic, Integrated Transformation Process

INTRODUCTION 215

TITLE OF TOOL

1. Finding Connections and Interrelationships Among the Five Whole Child Tenets. 217

2. School and District Profiles: What Can We Observe in Effective Whole Child Learning Organizations?. 221

3. Leadership in the Whole Child School. 225

4. Assessment and Evaluation in the Whole Child School 229

5. Technology and the Whole Child School. 235

6. The Whole Child "Walk-Through" Process—Suggested Procedures with Observation "Look-Fors". 241

7. The Whole Child Strategic Plan—A Sample Plan (Completed Example). 247

8. Checklist for Sustainng Momentum for Your Whole Child Initiative. 253

References and Other Resources. 257

The Whole Child Initiative as a Holistic, Integrated Transformation Process

Introduction

Each of the five tenets of the *Learning Compact Redefined* is necessary for a Whole Child school, yet they are insufficient in isolation. Similarly, the research-based best practices associated with achieving the commitments of each tenet are also interconnected. For example—

- The literature on high-quality health education clearly shows that students not only learn the knowledge, skills, and abilities they need to make good decisions about their health, but also learn cooperation, problem solving, decision making, and the health literacy skills needed for success in a global economy.
- Research shows that a challenging curriculum, positive school climate with high expectations, and good classroom management combine to offer students and adults a safe and supportive environment in which students feel connected to the school and the wider community. These types of schools include adults who act as mentors.
- Personalized learning and adult mentors are the hallmarks of quality service learning, a process that offers students real-world experiential learning opportunities and the ability to master 21st century educational and workplace skills, and reinforces sustained connections to the community.
- According to the Wingspread Declaration on School Connections, there is strong scientific evidence—across racial, ethnic, and income groups—that demonstrates that increased student connection to school promotes
  - educational motivation,
  - classroom engagement, and
  - improved school attendance.

Similarly, *The Whole Child: A Framework for Education in the 21st Century*, an ASCD Infobrief (Laitsch, Lewallen, & McClosky, 2005), emphasizes that meeting the needs of the whole child entails "providing a balanced curriculum, linking health needs with learning expectations, and ensuring fair and comprehensive assessments." These authors also emphasize how the arts and health affect academic achievement, the importance of civic and character education, the need for schools to engage students, and the pressures of high-stakes testing on educators' mission to educate the whole child.

The ASCD's *Learning Compact Redefined* emphasizes that our current, well-intentioned focus on academics is essential. Global economics require that each citizen be prepared to live in and contribute to a worldwide community of shrinking size and growing complexity. Additionally, the connection between in-school success and out-of-school context is strong and argues for schools and communities working together to put young people at the center of their decision making:

> Schools hold themselves accountable for ensuring that each student entrusted to them has the academic and cultural tools needed to succeed—and for creating a lifelong passion for learning. These schools have a clear understanding of what their students should know and be able to do and an even clearer understanding of how children and adolescents learn. No two students are the same, and the most successful schools and districts reflect this. (p. 11)

In *All Together Now: Sharing Responsibility for the Whole Child,* Blank and Berg (2006) suggest that nearly a century of research has come to one conclusion: Children develop along multiple, interconnected domains, and when one developmental domain is ignored, other domains may suffer (p. 6). Increasingly, research is showing that connecting all these factors (a safe, motivating environment; enrichment; and varied learning experiences) to the community yields enhanced results for every learner (p. 7).

This section will provide you with support and resources for use in your investigation of how the five Whole Child tenets interconnect and mutually support one another.

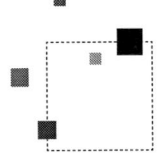

Action Tool One: Finding Connections and Interrelationships Among the Five Whole Child Tenets

PURPOSE OF THIS TOOL

A central and recurring theme in your work with the Whole Child Initiative is the need to help all participating stakeholders understand interconnections and relationships among the five Whole Child tenets. Your Whole Child strategic planning process should be holistic and integrated, rather than view each tenet as a separate silo. This tool articulates some important relationships between and among the five tenets.

HOW TO USE THIS TOOL

You can use this tool in a variety of contexts and situations. It is useful for start-up conversations about the five Whole Child tenets, especially as stakeholders start the strategic planning process. It can also be a useful resource for work with developing and implementing your Whole Child strategic plan. If you are integrating your Whole Child work into your existing school improvement plan, this resource can support your identification of key priorities.

TIPS AND VARIATIONS

- ✓ Review the ideas and recommendations presented here to refresh participants' understanding of the relationship among the five Whole Child tenets and the importance of maintaining a holistic vision and approach to change.
- ✓ Use the ideas and questions here as catalysts for debate and inquiry, including having stakeholders generate their own recommendations and ideas for cross-tenet relationships.
- ✓ Share the ideas presented here with students, asking them for suggestions about improvements and modifications they would like to see in your school community.

ActionTOOL

Finding Connections and Interrelationships Among the Five Whole Child Tenets

DIRECTIONS:

Use the following recommendations and suggestions for finding connections and relationships between the five Whole Child tenets. This tool can be especially useful for Whole Child strategic planning teams committed to reinforcing a holistic, unified portrait of their work with Whole Child tenets.

1. **Tenet One:** Each student enters school healthy and learns about and practices a healthy lifestyle.

   Potential areas of cross-tenet connection:

   - How will we determine how each student's physical health needs are being met and how those needs are affecting the student in such areas as intellectual challenge and engagement?
   - How will we determine how each student's choices about health and lifestyle issues affect their physical and emotional safety?
   - How will we explore how students' physical, emotional, and social well-being affect their sense of intellectual challenge and rigor in the classroom?
   - How can we determine if personalizing the learning process contributes to student health and emotional well-being?
   - How does working with qualified, caring adults enhance each student's physical and emotional well-being and sense of safety?
   - To what extent do students' healthy choices affect their preparation for postsecondary education and the world of work?

   Additional connections and ideas for integration:

Action Tool One: Finding Connections and Interrelationships
Among the Five Whole Child Tenets

2. **Tenet Two:** Each student learns in an intellectually challenging environment that is physically and emotionally safe for students and adults.

    Potential areas of cross-tenet connection:

    - How are intellectual challenge and students' physical and emotional well-being correlated or interconnected?
    - How can helping students make wise and healthy choices and decisions enhance their sense of engagement and intellectual challenge?
    - What does it mean to be emotionally safe? How can educators contribute to students' perception that learning environments are emotionally safe, challenging, and engaging?
    - How can personalizing the learning environment contribute to students' sense of intellectual challenge and engagement?
    - How are students' levels of intellectual challenge correlated with their preparation for postsecondary education and work?

    Additional connections and ideas for integration:

3. **Tenet Three:** Each student is actively engaged in learning and is connected to the school and broader community.

    Potential areas of cross-tenet connection:

    - How can the school and the broader community collaborate to ensure that each student is healthy and practices healthy lifestyle choices?
    - How will our emphasis upon intellectual challenge produce a more engaging learning environment for each student?
    - How will curriculum-related field experiences and other outreach initiatives increase our students' connections to both the school and the community?
    - How can we enlist active and sustained support from the broader community to enhance the physical and emotional safety of our school?
    - How will ensuring that each student is actively engaged in learning contribute to his or her ultimate success in postsecondary education and the world of work in the global environment?
    - Why does students' engagement in the learning process depend upon their understanding of authentic, real-world connections between learning and their world, including their local community?

    Additional connections and ideas for integration:

4. **Tenet Four:** Each student has access to personalized learning and to qualified, caring adults.

    Potential areas of cross-tenet connection:

    - How does being qualified, caring adults require us to view and approach each student holistically, including their physical, emotional, and social-relational needs and development?
    - How can we serve as role models for helping our students to understand and practice healthy lifestyle choices?
    - How would an increased emphasis on personalizing the learning environment contribute to our students' sense of intellectual challenge and rigor?
    - What can we do with preservice training (including cross-institutional partnerships with colleges of education) to enhance our ability to ensure that every newly hired staff member is highly qualified and certified?
    - How will emphasizing the need to display caring behaviors and attitudes among staff contribute to students' sense of emotional safety?

    Additional connections and ideas for integration:

5. **Tenet Five:** Each graduate is prepared for success in college or further study and for employment in a global environment.

    Potential areas of cross-tenet connection:

    - How might we collaborate with schools in our feeder patterns (i.e., elementary to middle to high school) to ensure that students are prepared for intellectually rigorous, challenging, and engaging academic coursework?
    - How can we ensure that elementary and middle schools prepare each student for success in academic coursework necessary for admission to postsecondary educational institutions?
    - How can we build consensus about cognitive and emotional competencies necessary for students' success in the world of work?
    - How can we improve all facets of our students' development to ensure that they are prepared for success in their futures?

    Additional connections and ideas for integration:

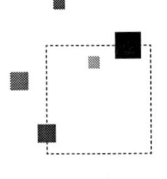

Action Tool Two: School and District Profiles: What Can We Observe in Effective Whole Child Learning Organizations?

PURPOSE OF THIS TOOL

Reinforcing the theme of discovering ways for schools and districts to create and realize a unified Whole Child vision, this tool contains a series of brief summaries highlighting successful Whole Child sites. The tool is organized according to how each site reflects success in a specific tenet. Reflect on how the site resonates and expresses its connection to each of the major tenets of the Whole Child Compact.

HOW TO USE THIS TOOL

Share these profiles in a variety of venues, including staff discussions, study group activities, and community meetings. Use the guide questions presented for each case study to shape initial conversations and discussions. Encourage participants to ask questions and make assertions that reflect their independent perspectives, ideas, and suggestions. At the conclusion of the organizational profiles, you will also find *Educational Leadership* articles and study group questions.

TIPS AND VARIATIONS

- ✓ Compare how your learning organization reflects aspects of the programs and practices described in each case study. Are there areas in which enhancements or improvements might be called for?
- ✓ JIGSAW the information presented here, with each expert team concentrating on one of the case study summaries. Then have participants return to their base team and have team members create a unified portrait of what the profiles suggest about overall Whole Child learning organizations.
- ✓ Incorporate ideas and suggestions from each profile into your own Whole Child planning process.
- ✓ Use the articles and guide questions presented at the conclusion of this tool as part of a study group formed to investigate cross-tenet connections and relationships.

School and District Profiles: What Can We Observe in Effective Whole Child Learning Organizations?

(from the ASCD Whole Child Compact document)

Tenet One: Entering School Healthy and Promoting Healthy Schools and Healthy Lifestyles

Communities worldwide have adopted a whole child–whole community approach. The Model Schools for Inner Cities Initiative in Toronto makes the school the hub of the community for education and community health. At the Yukon's Whitehorse Elementary, an innovative community partnership focuses on removing barriers to learning that stand outside the school walls. The United Kingdom's Priory Lane Junior School—designated as "outstanding" by Ofsted, the official inspectorate for children and learning in England—emphasizes both high expectations and developing social and emotional competency.

In the United States, the Illinois State Board of Education (ISBE) includes in its state learning standards performance indicators in the traditional academic areas assessed through the No Child Left Behind Act, and adds indicators for physical development and health, foreign language, fine arts, social and emotional learning, and measurements of the educational environment of each school.

The Interactive Illinois Report Card, an interactive Web site created at Northern Illinois University and funded by the ISBE, provides visitors with the accountability measures defined in the Illinois state learning standards, which include social and emotional learning. ISBE's social and emotional learning goals, standards, and benchmarks were developed by a broad-based group of educators, human services professionals, and parents, and they correlate with Illinois learning standards. Performance descriptors offer learning targets with greater detail.

Our analysis: What elements of Tenet One seem apparent here? What are the implications of this summary for our work with the Whole Child strategic planning process?

Tenet Two: Ensuring That Each Child Participates in Intellectually Challenging Learning Environments That Are Physically and Emotionally Safe

Price Laboratory School in Cedar Falls, Iowa, developed a Buddy Circles program to partner 4th grade students with their peers from a school for children with physical and mental disabilities. In a society where the term "retard" is used so often in a joking or put-down way, participants in the program collaborated to discover the many abilities people with disabilities have, learn to respect ways that people are similar and different, and reflect on the importance of friendship for all kids.

Postproject survey data (Struck, 2006) show they did just that:

- "I learned that even if you have disabilities everyone has emotions and you can still get hurt by other people."
- "It was like being with one of my friends except he couldn't talk as much and I had to push his wheelchair."

Our analysis: What elements of Tenet Two seem apparent here? What are the implications of this summary for our work with the Whole Child strategic planning process?

Tenet Three: Ensuring Active Student Engagement and Connectedness

Quest High School, outside of Houston, Texas, was established on the principles of shared leadership and shared decision making. Understanding of and commitment to education of the whole child is built into every policy. Students at Quest are actively involved in curriculum writing. They plan, assess, and monitor their own wellness plan, including elements of physical, social, and emotional health, and complete their studies with a research-based social action plan. Character education and civic responsibility are not just part of the curriculum, but part of the students' lives through the structure of the school. Teachers use the title "facilitator" and lead "families" of 20–25 students in "houses" rather than classrooms. Families meet daily and students remain in the same family over four years, helping students develop interpersonal skills that enhance their success in academics and other areas.

As one student put it, "Quest has helped me to take time to think about what I'm learning. Quest does make me think and learn instead of memorizing just to forget a week later. Above that, my actual character has improved. I don't feel awkward, and I have a lot of confidence in myself. I am more responsible as well." Quest is the highest-rated high school in its district, receiving the second-highest level of recognition on Texas' school accountability measure in 2006.

New Hampshire has embarked on a large-scale effort to transform teaching and learning practices in its schools. The state's comprehensive education reform plan is grounded in a commitment to effectively incorporate real-world learning into the fabric of New Hampshire's public schools. In practice, New Hampshire's schools are increasingly using partners beyond the schoolhouse—local organizations, businesses, and government agencies—to educate children. The strategies move a step beyond the practice of sending students outside the school door to engage in periodic learning at local community sites. Embedded in New Hampshire's vision is an open-door policy that allows community members to enter as trusted educators while students exit for class credits earned in real-world settings. In this model, the local museum curator becomes a purveyor of art and history knowledge, afternoon gymnastics classes are counted as credit for physical education requirement, and the researcher at the local aquarium is the science teacher for two days a week. New Hampshire's model of schooling demands statewide understanding of and agreement to expectations and outcomes for its children.

Our analysis: What elements of Tenet Three seem apparent here? What are the implications of this summary for our work with the Whole Child strategic planning process?

Tenet Four: Personalizing the Learning Process and Ensuring All Learners Work with Qualified, Caring Adults

In Long Beach, California, Stevenson-YMCA Community School works with community-based organizations and parents to develop students' social, emotional, physical, moral, and academic competencies. The YMCA acts as a lead partner, providing resources and space and hiring a community school coordinator. Community and student leadership institutes, after-school enrichment, and adult education classes—many led by residents—are at the heart of the community school. Mental health services are available on-site, and the school has a close relationship with a nearby community health center, which provides medical services. The principal is convinced that the school must pay attention to the whole child to help students succeed academically. And the results bear out this belief: Stevenson is meeting adequate yearly progress goals and has been designated a California Distinguished School.

Our analysis: What elements of Tenet Four seem apparent here? What are the implications of this summary for our work with the Whole Child strategic planning process?

Tenet Five: Preparing Each Student for College and Postgraduation Study and Work in a Global Environment

Facing challenges in providing education to an increasingly ethnically and socioeconomically diverse student body from several neighboring communities, Hand Middle School in Columbia, South Carolina, restructured its curriculum and approaches to learning. The result was a new schoolwide, arts-focused learning community with strong learning partnerships between the arts and education. Each grade is divided into smaller teams of 100–125 students, and students spend the school year focused on a theme that frames their course content. Parents, teachers, and administrators together choose a schoolwide theme to guide the academic year. Since the transformation, Hand has seen an 85 percent increase in academic performance, and in 2004 it was named one of only five Creative Ticket National Schools of Distinction by the Kennedy Center for the Performing Arts.

Hamilton County Public Schools in Chattanooga, Tennessee, have experienced a remarkable turnaround: dramatic reading gains in urban elementary schools, more challenging and engaging high schools, and better-trained teachers and leaders. In 2000, only 18 percent of 3rd graders were reading at or above grade level, and the district had nine of the lowest-performing elementary schools in the state. By 2006, 74 percent of students tested proficient or advanced in reading, and the once-failing schools outgained more than 90 percent of all schools in Tennessee.

In 2001, Hamilton County Public Schools received an $8 million grant from the Carnegie Corporation of New York's New Schools for a New Society. The Chattanooga Public Education Fund committed to raising a matching $6 million for high school reform. Hamilton adopted a key strategy: a single-path diploma for all students that raises graduation rates and prepares students for four-year college or a higher-skill job. Each school developed its own reform blueprint while addressing four basic goals: creating a more challenging, relevant, and engaging curriculum; improving teaching by providing more professional development; providing a more personalized and engaging experience for students; and maintaining flexibility in meeting student needs more effectively.

Eleven high schools have career academies, including business, technology, engineering, environmental sciences, global studies, transportation, health sciences, and construction. Some schools host several academies. All academies combine college preparatory work with a career theme to make academic learning more relevant and challenging. All schools have a summer transition program for 9th graders, and some are creating 9th grade academies that give students more individual attention in this critical year.

Our analysis: What elements of Tenet Five seem apparent here? What are the implications of this summary for our work with the Whole Child strategic planning process?

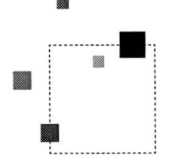

Action Tool Three: Leadership in the Whole Child School

PURPOSE OF THIS TOOL

Leadership in Whole Child schools is distributed, with administrators conveying authority and power to teacher leaders, community stakeholders, and other individuals whose expertise can best lead and guide reform initiatives. Although traditional policy-based leadership roles will remain, the goal of effective Whole Child leadership is collaborative inquiry and stakeholder empowerment aligned with the principles and strategies of the five Whole Child tenets.

HOW TO USE THIS TOOL

This tool is designed for use by a variety of individuals and groups interested in discussing and exploring the implications of the Whole Child Compact for educational leadership. An administrator can use it to reflect on how he or she is displaying the characteristics and behaviors of an effective Whole Child leader. Teacher leaders can use it independently or with other educators to reflect on their vision and goals for effective school-based leadership. Finally, this tool can be shared with families and community stakeholders interested in understanding how leadership should function in a Whole Child context.

TIPS AND VARIATIONS

- ✓ Compare the recommendations presented in this action tool to traditional leadership standards and expectations. How are they similar? How do they differ?
- ✓ Use this tool as part of a preleadership development program, encouraging prospective administrators to consider how they might demonstrate the behaviors identified here.

Leadership in the Whole Child School

DIRECTIONS:

Use this tool to assess your own leadership style or to reflect on educational leaders with whom you are familiar. To what extent does each of them demonstrate the priorities and behaviors identified here? In your opinion, why is each behavior considered essential to effective Whole Child leadership? Consider the following rating scale for each trait or focus area: 4 = Highly evident at all times; 3 = Generally evident with some omissions; 2 = Evident to some degree but needs more emphasis; 1 = Generally absent and requires much more emphasis; 0 = Missing and requires immediate long-term emphasis.

Recommended Leadership Trait/Priority—An Effective Whole Child Leader—	Rating
1. Clearly understands the concept of educating the whole child.	4 3 2 1 0
2. Can explain the major tenets and their implications for educating the whole child.	4 3 2 1 0
3. Is committed to the principles of equity and rigor, ensuring that every student is successful.	4 3 2 1 0
4. Works collaboratively with other educators to ensure that every child enters school healthy.	4 3 2 1 0
5. Promotes healthy conditions within the school, including policy- and legally mandated structures and processes within the physical plant.	4 3 2 1 0
6. Promotes staff members' awareness of the need to model and reinforce for students healthy choices and healthy decision-making processes.	4 3 2 1 0
7. Provides meaningful and sustained instructional leadership to ensure that curriculum is standards driven and that instruction reflects intellectual challenge for every learner.	4 3 2 1 0
8. Collaborates with staff to ensure that every classroom and the school as a whole is physically and emotionally safe for all participants in the learning community.	4 3 2 1 0
9. Observes and coaches teachers to ensure that the instruction they provide engages every student.	4 3 2 1 0
10. Works with all stakeholders to ensure that every learner feels connected to the classroom, school, and community.	4 3 2 1 0
11. Ensures that financial and scheduling resources are available to help every staff member be a qualified and caring educator.	4 3 2 1 0
12. Understands and supports collaborative inquiry in the form of opportunities for all staff members to engage in lesson study, study groups, inquiry teams, and action research projects.	4 3 2 1 0
13. Provides oversight of the curriculum and instructional programs offered to ensure that they are rigorous and challenging enough to help every student prepare for postsecondary education.	4 3 2 1 0
14. Works with all staff members to help every student identify and prepare for meaningful career pathways associated with the global environment.	4 3 2 1 0
15. Encourages school-based budgeting (as permitted by the district) so that financial resources are available to support identified Whole Child priorities.	4 3 2 1 0

Recommended Leadership Trait/Priority—(continued) An Effective Whole Child Leader—	Rating
16. Collaborates with other educators within the school to ensure that newly hired staff members have appropriate certification, a rigorous educational background, and a caring temperament in their interactions with all students.	4　3　2　1　0
17. Understands and promotes stakeholder involvement in day-to-day school operations as well as governance and management, where appropriate.	4　3　2　1　0
18. Works with staff to develop and implement community outreach and family training opportunities to maximize the achievement of every student.	4　3　2　1　0
19. Understands the value of and promotes the development of cross-institutional partnerships aligned with Whole Child priorities and long-range goals.	4　3　2　1　0
20. Reinforces shared/distributed leadership in the development and implementation of the school's Whole Child strategic plan.	4　3　2　1　0

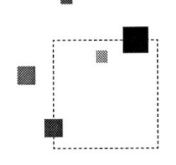

Action Tool Four: Assessment and Evaluation in the Whole Child School

PURPOSE OF THIS TOOL

Determining the impact of your Whole Child work is a critical part of your strategic planning process. This tool distinguishes between two important and interrelated processes that should support your work. The first is assessment, which we define as collecting and analyzing student achievement and performance data to make adjustments, provide on-the-spot feedback, and support each student in moving along a developmental continuum. The second is evaluation, which requires the identification and application of performance standards to make judgments about the quality and effectiveness of student work products and processes as well as organizational effectiveness and related performance gaps. This tool is designed to place both processes within the context of the Whole Child strategic improvement process.

HOW TO USE THIS TOOL

Use this tool as a springboard and catalyst for reflecting on current assessment and evaluation practices and processes in your school or district. While the principles underlying each of the criteria identified here are universal best practices according to contemporary educational research, they are also extremely important in sustaining your work with the Whole Child Initiative. Identify areas in which there is a high level of use of each strategy and process. Also consider areas in which there may be underutilization of suggested practices—and the implications of those gaps for achieving your vision and goals for educating the whole child.

TIPS AND VARIATIONS

- ✓ You might consider using the recommendations presented in this tool as a basis for designing assessment and evaluation professional development sessions in your school or district.
- ✓ Encourage staff members to consider not only their current use of identified assessment and evaluation practices, but also the implications of a failure to use them. For example, what is missing in your Whole Child strategic plan? What are you not able to discern or monitor if one or more of these recommended practices is absent in your learning organization?

Assessment and Evaluation in the Whole Child School

Directions: Read each assessment component. If the component is already in place, list strategies and practices currently used to support this component. If the component is not in place or needs improvement, list suggestions for how this component could be implemented or strengthened in your school.

Diagnostic Assessment	Strategies/Practices Already in Place	Suggestions for Improvement/ Implementation
At the beginning of instructional episodes, units, and grading periods, we diagnose students' readiness levels, interests, and learning profiles.		
We provide immediate and ongoing feedback and coaching to every student based on his or her diagnosed levels of competency in relation to content and performance standards.		
We articulate levels of proficiency for each learning standard so that each student can self-monitor and self-evaluate.		

Formative Assessment	Strategies/Practices Already in Place	Suggestions for Improvement/ Implementation
Throughout a lesson, unit, and grading period, we use formal and informal data collection and analysis methods to provide ongoing and immediate feedback to every student.		
Through our formative assessment system, students are actively involved in their own assessment and evaluation processes, monitoring and recording their progress in relation to each content and performance standard.		
Formative assessment is generally not graded, so that students can revisit and revise their own learning as they prepare for formal summative assessment tasks.		
We use a range of formative assessment strategies, including journals, logs, interviews, observations, exit slips, informal and formal performance tasks, and academic prompts.		
We communicate levels of standards proficiency to students via rubrics, which they are encouraged to use for self-monitoring and peer coaching.		

Summative Assessment	Strategies/Practices Already in Place	Suggestions for Improvement/ Implementation
There is a close and sustained alignment between our formative assessment practices and the summative assessments students are asked to complete.		
We use a balanced approach to summative assessment, avoiding exclusive dependence on formal tests and quizzes in favor of a range of assessment tasks.		
Our range of summative assessment tasks includes tests and quizzes that have constructed-response items; academic prompts; authentic performance tasks; and culminating projects, performances, and presentations.		
All summative assessments are scored with clearly articulated rubrics or scoring guides so that students are clear about the alignment between the assessment and the standards they were responsible for mastering.		
Grading is based on students' standards mastery.		

Summative Assessment (continued)	Strategies/Practices Already in Place	Suggestions for Improvement/ Implementation
We have eliminated traditional grading issues and problems (e.g., the undue influence of the "zero" grade, failure to reward cumulative progress by overemphasizing students' initial grades during a grading period).		

Evaluation	Strategies/Practices Already in Place	Suggestions for Improvement/ Implementation
We have clearly identified our curriculum content standards.		
Our curriculum content standards are guaranteed and viable, ensuring that instructors have sufficient time to help every student master them.		
We have identified levels of proficiency (advanced, proficient, developing, minimal, absent) for each of our major content standards.		
We communicate levels of proficiency to our students so that they can monitor and adjust their learning processes in relation to each standard.		

Evaluation (continued)	Strategies/Practices Already in Place	Suggestions for Improvement/ Implementation
For every content standard, we have identified appropriate performance standards (performance indicators) for each grade level so that we can monitor students' annual progress.		
We determine the value added to our instructional programs based on longitudinal performance of each student relative to our content and performance standards.		
We emphasize all aspects of our students' development in delineating our content and performance standards, including longitudinal monitoring of students' academic and intellectual growth, their emotional development, and their social-behavioral growth.		
We conduct formal and longitudinal program evaluations on key elements of the five Whole Child tenets, including evaluating student progress in relation to them.		
We conduct formal and longitudinal program evaluations related to key organizational practices and human resources, including evaluating our progress in and the impact of Whole Child focus areas.		

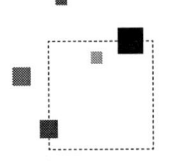

Action Tool Five: Technology and the Whole Child School

PURPOSE OF THIS TOOL

The breathtaking transformations occurring as a result of technology are frequently underemphasized or not acknowledged in many schools. In a Whole Child school, however, technology should be in the forefront, promoting students' active learning process; encouraging investigation and inquiry; and complementing research-based best practices in curriculum, assessment, and the teaching-learning partnership. This tool provides an overview of the recurrent conditions and principles emphasized in successful Whole Child learning organizations.

HOW TO USE THIS TOOL

This tool is not meant to be comprehensive in its delineation of technology requirements and recommendations within the Whole Child strategic planning process. Instead, it should be considered a list of provocations for discussion and exploration. To what extent, for example, do you use technology to support student learning? How do you update your technology-based infrastructure? Perhaps most significant, how do you address the growing impact of technology on students' thinking and learning processes?

TIPS AND VARIATIONS

- ✓ Consider ways to incorporate the suggestions in this tool into your Whole Child strategic planning process. For example, could a study group begin an initial exploration of how technology should best be used to complement and personalize each student's learning process?
- ✓ You might also decide to incorporate the recommendations in this tool into your walk-through and observation process (described in detail in the next action tool in this section).
- ✓ Incorporate the articles included in this section (available to you online using the pass code assigned with the purchase of this ASCD action tool) into study group work.
- ✓ Explore action research projects involving one or more aspects of technology to personalize learning for every student and to challenge students preparing for the world of the 21st century.

Technology and the Whole Child School

INTRODUCTION

Consider the recommendations presented below for your work with each of the Whole Child tenets. As you discuss each recommendation, how would you rate your school or district's current level of use for each indicator?

- 4 = High level of use in all areas
- 3 = High level of use in some areas but needs attention in others
- 2 = Some level of use in certain areas but absent in many areas
- 1 = Generally absent in most areas of our school
- 0 = Totally absent in all areas of our school

General Principles: The following operating principles are essential for the Whole Child school:

1. We are committed to keeping up-to-date about electronic, multimedia, and related forms of technology that can enhance each of our students' growth and development.
2. We ensure that technology is integrated successfully into all classrooms, complementing the teaching-learning process.
3. We continue to assess and evaluate each student's growth in understanding and using technology, monitoring their progress along a developmental continuum using clearly articulated standards and levels of proficiency organized according to competency (from advanced to proficient to developing to emerging).
4. We maximize our school's use of technology to accommodate the unique strengths and needs (physical, academic-intellectual, social-emotional, behavioral) of each of our students, ensuring active data collection and analysis.
5. We ensure that every staff member is qualified to use a range of technologies in his or her position, including as a key resource in curriculum, assessment, and the teaching-learning process.
6. Our physical plant(s) are up-to-date and ensure that every student has access to a range of technologies to support their education.

Implications for our school or district:

Action Tool Five: Technology and the Whole Child School

Tenet One: Technology, Healthy Students and Staff, Healthy Schools, and Healthy Lifestyles

- We use a range of technologies to monitor students' health, including data related to their levels of health as they enter school (e.g., immunization, physical checkups).
- We use technology to inform our preK–12 students to help them understand the significance of nutrition upon our health and well-being.
- Technology helps us to reinforce physical exercise programs that support a healthy lifestyle for students and staff.
- We use a range of technologies (including our Web site, Web pages, and teacher-facilitated electronic forums) to support staff and students' development of healthy behaviors.
- We update our staff and student understanding of physical health, nutrition, and fitness regimens via a range of electronic information dissemination. This process includes the Internet, intranet, and other electronic media for disseminating research-based ideas and information about healthy living and healthy lifestyles.

Implications for our school or district:

Tenet Two: Technology, Intellectual Challenge, and Physically and Emotionally Safe Learning Environments

- Whenever possible, we integrate technology-driven or technology-based scenarios, simulations, case studies, and related activities and tasks to enhance students' sense of intellectual challenge.
- We periodically use technology to conduct cross-student, cross-school dialogues and forums on curriculum-related content.
- Where feasible, we use online coursework in our classrooms as well as in our ongoing professional development.
- We use technology (e.g., computer stations, electronic projection devices, electronic voting and feedback systems) to enhance students' sense of intellectual engagement and challenge in each classroom.
- We keep up-to-date electronic records and databases of relevant data concerning the physical and emotional safety of our learning environment.

Implications for our school or district:

Tenet Three: Technology, Active Student Engagement, and Connectedness to the School and the Community

- We balance whole-class, teacher-directed learning with a range of cooperative learning and independent tasks and enhance student engagement via appropriate and timely uses of technology.
- We use a range of electronic resources to build a sense of community within the classroom, school, and the community.
- We take advantage of online searches, Web sites, and related technology-based resources to promote students' sense of academic engagement and connectedness.
- We integrate technology into cooperative learning activities to promote student connectivity and interdependence.
- We maximize our use of technology as part of our in-class and schoolwide assessment system, encouraging students to create electronic portfolios to store work products, learning artifacts, and self-reflections.
- Electronic grading enables us to help students keep abreast of how they are progressing with each academic standard.
- We promote family and community engagement and connectivity via class Web sites, posting homework assignments and course/grade-level outlines, and so forth.

Implications for our school or district:

Tenet Four: Technology, Personalizing the Learning Environment, and Ensuring Qualified, Caring Adults

- We use technology to personalize the learning environment for every student, including electronic voting and other resources to allow teachers to receive immediate feedback from students related to their levels of understanding and use of key curriculum concepts, ideas, skills, and procedures.
- Technology plays an ongoing and effective role in our approach to differentiation, ensuring that individual students' readiness levels, interests, and learning profiles are accommodated.
- We use technology to enhance our approach to professional development, including providing online coursework for teachers to update certification requirements.
- As part of our study group, inquiry team, and action research projects, staff can access internal Web sites for updates and to learn from one another.

Implications for our school or district:

Tenet Five: Technology and Preparation of Students for Postsecondary Education and the World of Work in the 21st Century

- We use technology as a focus of our curriculum content's meta-skills, including monitoring students' growing technology literacy, increasing competency in information acquisition and evaluation, and evolving proficiency in using a range of technologies for practice of core skills as well as real-world problem solving and decision making,
- We encourage our students to use technology-based formats in formal presentations and performances as part of their work with culminating performance tasks and projects.
- Our infrastructure supports the active and sustained use of technology in all content areas, including science, foreign languages, and the visual and performing arts.
- We carefully integrate our work with career development and career pathways for every student, including guidance counselor databases, lists of Web sites for information searches, and direct training of students in career-related technology skills and competencies.
- Our community outreach and engagement activities for Tenet Five emphasize stakeholder access to and use of key technologies to support student preparation for postsecondary education and careers.

Implications for our school or district:

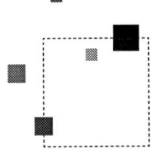

Action Tool Six: The Whole Child "Walk-Through" Process—Suggested Procedures with Observation "Look-Fors"

PURPOSE OF THIS TOOL

What should you be able to observe during a Whole Child walk-through process? This tool is designed to answer that question by providing walk-through teams with a set of observation criteria related to each of the Whole Child tenets. Generally, the walk-through process is designed to capture a kind of photograph of a point in time within the learning organization. Ideally, follow-up walk-throughs would be conducted to observe organizational performance over time. Also, walk-through data are used for whole-staff feedback rather than individual staff observations. Walk-through teams are engaged in a kind of anthropological research, discerning observable patterns and group behaviors with the overall learning organization or subcomponents of it.

HOW TO USE THIS TOOL

No individual walk-through team should be expected to observe for all of the performance indicators included with this action tool. Instead, consider having a series of walk-through processes conducted at different times by different observers. Each walk-through might be devoted to one aspect of the Whole Child set of performance indicators. Follow-up sessions can be conducted to triangulate initial data and related observer conclusions about observable patterns. Walk-throughs are valuable resources for inclusion in your school improvement or strategic planning process.

TIPS AND VARIATIONS

- ✓ Invite external observers from your central office as well as community stakeholders to form walk-through observation teams for a specific tenet or subcomponents of it. Have observers present their observations and conclusions to the staff as soon as possible after the completion of their work.
- ✓ Consider forming peer-based walk-through teams responsible for observing and analyzing data patterns related to a significant aspect of your Whole Child strategic plan. For example, have a small group of peers move through classrooms during a two-hour period to observe for student engagement, intellectual challenge, or related indicators of a rigorous curriculum and instructional program.
- ✓ Use the walk-through process to collect data on phenomena for which you may not already have formalized evaluation standards or processes. For example, this protocol can be used to discern levels of caring on the part of staff members. It can also be an ideal method for analyzing levels of emotional safety within a building.

The Whole Child "Walk-Through" Process—Suggested Procedures with Observation "Look-Fors"

Whole Child Look-Fors				
Tenet One	**1** (Not Present)	**2** (Inconsistent or in Need of Enhancement)	**3** (Consistently Present)	**4** (Consistently Present with Advanced Enhancements)
1. There is a high level of student health and well-being.				
2. The school promotes student and staff health.				
3. There are conditions present that confirm the school is a healthy building and learning organization.				
4. Students make healthy choices.				
5. Staff models and practices healthy decision making.				
6. There are high levels of physical safety within the building.				
7. There is evidence of organizational conformity to policy and legislative mandates for healthy and safe environments.				

Whole Child Look-Fors

Tenet Two	1 (Not Present)	2 (Inconsistent or in Need of Enhancement)	3 (Consistently Present)	4 (Consistently Present with Advanced Enhancements)
1. Each student experiences learning as intellectually challenging.				
2. Intellectual challenge is not threatening or counterproductive for any student.				
3. Instructional strategies are clearly aligned with well-articulated content and performance standards.				
4. Instructional practices are designed to challenge each student while accommodating their individual readiness levels.				
5. Instructional practices are designed to challenge each student while addressing their individual learning profiles.				
6. Instructional practices are designed to challenge each student while addressing their interests, when feasible.				
7. The learning environment in each classroom, hallway, and other school area is physically safe for every student and staff member.				
8. The learning environment in each classroom, hallway, and other area of the school is emotionally safe for every student and staff member.				

Whole Child Look-Fors				
Tenet Three	**1** (Not Present)	**2** (Inconsistent or in Need of Enhancement)	**3** (Consistently Present)	**4** (Consistently Present with Advanced Enhancements)
1. Each student is actively engaged in the learning process.				
2. The teacher promotes student engagement through a variety of instructional practices.				
3. Each student is positively engaged with the curriculum content he or she is studying.				
4. Each student is positively engaged with peers.				
5. Each student is positively engaged with the instructor.				

Action Tool Six: The Whole Child "Walk-Through" Process—Suggested Procedures with Observation "Look-Fors"

Whole Child Look-Fors				
Tenet Four	**1** (Not Present)	**2** (Inconsistent or in Need of Enhancement)	**3** (Consistently Present)	**4** (Consistently Present with Advanced Enhancements)
1. The learning process is regularly personalized for every student.				
2. The instructor has a sound and fluent understanding of the content being taught.				
3. The instructor demonstrates a sound and consistent knowledge of effective pedagogy.				
4. The instructor demonstrates a solid understanding of the key strategies related to differentiated instruction.				
5. Each staff member demonstrates appropriate caring and concern for the students with whom they interact (both within and outside the classroom).				

Whole Child Look-Fors				
Tenet Five	**1** (Not Present)	**2** (Inconsistent or in Need of Enhancement)	**3** (Consistently Present)	**4** (Consistently Present with Advanced Enhancements)
1. All areas of the curriculum promote every student's preparation for postsecondary education.				
2. When feasible, correlations and connections are made between students' academic learning and their preparation for the 21st century global environment.				
3. There is emphasis on instructional and learning activities that reinforce students' metacognitive skills and competencies.				
4. Every student has the opportunity to complete a rigorous range of curriculum offerings, including foreign language, the visual and performing arts, social studies, and experimental science.				
5. The curriculum is globally focused and emphasizes ongoing comparisons of perspectives and points of view.				

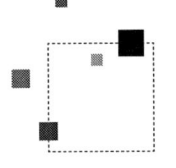

Action Tool Seven: The Whole Child Strategic Plan—A Sample Plan (Completed Example)

PURPOSE OF THIS TOOL

For each of the sections in this ASCD action tool devoted to specific Whole Child tenets, you have examined suggested strategic planning elements presented in a strategic planning template. As you begin to synthesize and consolidate your efforts, you may wish to examine the completed example of a school's Whole Child strategic plan.

HOW TO USE THIS TOOL

This sample completed strategic plan represents a hypothetical school's work with three key elements of the Whole Child Compact: (1) ensuring that each child learns in an intellectually challenging environment, (2) promoting physical safety within the school as a learning organization, and (3) promoting emotional safety within the school as a learning organization. The tool is designed to answer inevitable questions about what a Whole Child strategic plan might look like and how various Whole Child focus areas can be integrated and aligned.

TIPS AND VARIATIONS

- ✓ Although the school itself is hypothetical, the components of this plan can support your Whole Child work in two ways: (1) If you have elected to organize your Whole Child transformation work as a discrete process, you can use this example as a prototype for developing your own Whole Child strategic plan. (2) If you have chosen to integrate your Whole Child work into your existing school improvement plan, you can use the ideas and models presented here to guide that integration process.
- ✓ You may also elect to use this strategic plan as a discussion point as part of your professional development work with the Whole Child Initiative. A faculty meeting, for example, might be devoted to analyzing how the plan aligns with your school's current improvement planning process and how that process might be enhanced by emphasis upon Whole Child focus areas.

The Whole Child Strategic Plan—A Sample Plan (Completed Example)

A Sample Whole Child Strategic Plan for _____ School
Part I: Our Vision Statement
As a result of our commitment to the concept of educating the whole child, every student in our school will experience his or her learning environment as intellectually engaging as well as physically and emotionally safe.
Part II: Long-Range (Multiyear) Goals
1. Student Achievement Long-Range Goals: • Each child experiences intellectual challenge in every classroom. • Each child learns in a physically healthy environment that supports his or her academic, social, and emotional growth and development. • Each child learns in an emotionally safe environment conducive to intellectual rigor, engagement, motivation, and efficacy. 2. Staff Members' Long-Range Goals: • Ensure that every classroom is intellectually challenging for every student. • Ensure that the classroom and school are physically safe for every student. • Ensure that the classroom and school are emotionally safe for every student. 3. Administrative Long-Range Goals: • Ensure that all classrooms are intellectually challenging for every student. • Ensure that all classrooms and the school are physically safe for every student and staff member. • Ensure that the classroom and school are emotionally safe for every student and staff member.
Part III: Annual Performance Targets **From August 2009–June 2010:**
• Increase levels of observable intellectual challenge indicators in each classroom by a minimum of 25 percent (using staff-generated observation checklist). • Increase aggregate and disaggregated student grade point averages by a minimum of 10 percent. • Increase climate survey results in areas of intellectual challenge, physical safety, and emotional safety by a minimum of 20 percent. • Reduce student referrals by a minimum of 15 percent. • Reduce student suspensions and expulsions by a minimum of 20 percent.

A Sample Whole Child Strategic Plan (continued)

Part IV: Suggested Data Sources

- Attendance (including individuals and subgroups)
- Grade point averages (including individuals and subgroups)
- Academic achievement on standardized test scores (including individuals and subgroups)
- Levels of observable student intellectual challenge (e.g., aggregate and disaggregated data from walk-through processes, administrative observations, student questionnaires, climate surveys, focus group feedback)
- Participation of each student in appropriate physical activity
- Data related to quality of physical education experiences
- School climate surveys
- Survey, questionnaire, and focus group data generated from relevant stakeholders regarding physical and emotional conditions of the learning environment(s)
- External confirmation of school environmental conditions and alignment with district and other public policies and legislation
- Analysis and evaluation of health, nutrition, and physical activity resources available to students and families (e.g., levels of insurance coverage, access to in-school health services, vision and hearing screenings, ease of access to needed outside health and human services agencies)
- Suggestions for disaggregation of data (e.g., via analysis of subgroup patterns such as race, ethnicity, gender, socioeconomic status, region/community, special program status)
- Analysis of staff members' health and well-being (e.g., absentee rates, quality of health, related healthy lifestyle choices)

Part V: Action Plan
Suggested Time Line with Benchmark Deadlines:

1. By August 15, 2009, provide professional development sessions for each staff member on research-based best practices related to promoting students' sense of intellectual challenge, rigor, and physical and emotional safety.
2. By September 1, 2009, administer and analyze aggregate and disaggregated data results from a climate survey to be taken by all relevant stakeholder groups (e.g., students, staff, families, community members).
3. Subsequent to initial workshops (by September 15, 2009), finalize a consensus-driven checklist for observing intellectual challenge and physical and emotional safety in the school and classrooms.
4. By September 15, 2009, integrate climate survey and related stakeholder feedback into a preliminary needs analysis report to be presented at Back-to-School Night.
5. On a monthly basis, conduct walk-throughs and informal observations using consensus-driven checklist; gather and present to staff and other stakeholders longitudinal data concerning data patterns and gains in identified areas.
6. Beginning in November 2009, develop and implement a series of collaborative inquiry professional development processes (i.e., study groups, inquiry teams, and action research projects) to address identified areas of need. Throughout the academic year, have members of these groups present updates to the faculty and other stakeholder groups.
7. By January 2010, develop and implement community outreach and engagement activities and processes designed to support our achievement of our long-range goals and annual performance targets.
8. Continue throughout this academic year to determine the impact of interventions extending from the processes identified above.
9. Continue to modify our strategic plan to accommodate recommendations and suggestions emerging from collaborative teams and stakeholder groups.
10. During the last faculty meeting in June 2010, present summary report highlighting accomplishments and value added of our Whole Child intervention process.

A Sample Whole Child Strategic Plan (continued)

Part V: Action Plan (continued)

Suggestions for Determining Value Added of Our Whole Child Programs and Interventions:

- Increased levels of positive ratings during classroom observations and walk-through processes using checklists for the following criteria: intellectual challenge, physical safety, and emotional safety
- Reduced levels of incident reports (e.g., referrals, suspensions, expulsions)
- Increased positive ratings on school climate surveys
- Positive aggregate and disaggregated feedback patterns from focus group sessions on school climate and intellectual challenge
- Increased levels of student achievement data (e.g., grade point averages, standardized test data)

Individuals/Groups Responsible for Leadership and Facilitation:

- Self-identified staff interested in participating in initial study group activities
- Administrators assigned to facilitate development of key elements of the action plan
- Teacher leaders interested in key aspects of action plan focus areas
- Volunteer family and community members to serve on committees and related Whole Child activities

Part VI: Professional Development Plan

- Formal professional development to support staff understanding of research-based strategies and practices that promote intellectual challenge, physical safety, and emotional safety for all members of the learning community.
- A minimum of three study groups concentrating on (1) ways to promote intellectual challenge for every student, (2) ways to promote physical safety within the school and classrooms, and (3) ways to promote emotional safety within the school and classrooms.
- A minimum of three inquiry teams, extending from the initial work of study groups. NOTE: Participants may elect to recommend that initial study groups be fused into collaborative inquiry teams (e.g., working together to identify problems and issues related to general safety and ways specific physical and emotional safety concerns might be addressed).
- Small-group action research projects involving interested staff members who wish to identify hypothetical interventions for a specific problem or issue (identified by inquiry teams) and research how those interventions ameliorate the problem or issue.
- Projected costs: Each group or team will submit a preliminary projected budget to the administrator in charge requesting financing for needed materials, technology, substitute coverage, and so forth.
- Related resources: To be determined by each professional development inquiry team as part of its budget submission.
- Suggestions for program evaluation and value-added studies: As study groups and inquiry teams complete their initial work, they will be responsible for presenting a written and oral presentation summarizing their work, insights, and recommendations. Formal value-added evaluation is built into the protocol for action research projects.

Part VII: Community Outreach and Engagement

- Develop cross-institutional partnerships with local universities to help staff members in specific content areas keep informed about (1) changes in content focus, (2) research updates in key academic areas, and (3) collaboration on ways to better prepare students for success in key content areas at the postsecondary level.
- Conduct family training sessions: How can families help their children feel intellectually engaged in their education? How can families work with the school to ensure that their children are physically safe? How can families help the school to ensure that their children feel emotionally safe?
- Explore ways to engage community stakeholder individuals, groups, and organizations to expand availability of curriculum-related outreach activities and enrichment opportunities.

A Sample Whole Child Strategic Plan (continued)

Part VIII: Suggestions for Cross-Tenet Alignment

Our Whole Child strategic plan tends to emphasize Tenet Two (i.e., ensuring that every child experiences the learning environment as intellectually challenging and that every child and adult in the school feels physically and emotionally safe). As part of our plan, we need to consider the following questions and recommendations related to the four other Whole Child tenets:

- **Tenet One:** Each student enters school healthy and learns about and practices a healthy lifestyle. We need to determine how each student's physical health needs are being met and how their choices about health and lifestyle issues affect their physical and emotional safety. We also need to explore how students' physical well-being affects their sense of intellectual challenge and rigor in the classroom.
- **Tenet Three:** Each student is actively engaged in learning and is connected to the school and broader community. How will our emphasis on intellectual challenge produce a more engaging learning environment for each student? How will curriculum-related field experiences and other outreach initiatives increase our students' connections to both the school and the community? How can we enlist active and sustained community support from the broader community to enhance the physical and emotional safety of our school?
- **Tenet Four:** Each student has access to personalized learning and to qualified, caring adults. How would an increased emphasis upon personalizing the learning environment contribute to our students' sense of intellectual challenge and rigor? What can we do with preservice training (including cross-institutional partnerships with colleges of education) to enhance our ability to ensure that every newly hired staff member is highly qualified and certified? How will emphasizing the need to display caring behaviors and attitudes among staff contribute to students' sense of emotional safety?
- **Tenet Five:** Each graduate is prepared for success in college or further study and for employment in a global environment. How might we collaborate with schools in our feeder patterns (i.e., elementary to middle to high school) to ensure that students are prepared for intellectually rigorous, challenging, and engaging academic coursework? How can we ensure that elementary and middle schools prepare each student for success in academic coursework necessary for admission to postsecondary educational institutions? How can we build consensus about cognitive and emotional competencies necessary for students' success in the world of work?

Part IX: Potential Service Learning Projects

General Service Learning Project Suggestions

- Identify service learning projects that can complement students' display of ethical citizenship behaviors, emphasizing service to the school as a whole.

Content-Specific Service Learning Projects:

- Identify key areas of your curriculum in which service learning can become a useful and intellectually challenging venue for students to reinforce and extend their understanding of key concepts and generalizations from the material they study.

Level-Specific Service Learning Projects:

- Students within an overall grade level can collaborate on broader service learning activities and projects that reinforce such competencies as team-based decision making, problem solving, technology application, and critical thinking.

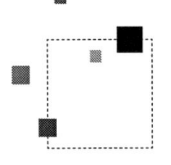

Action Tool Eight: Checklist for Sustaining Momentum for Your Whole Child Initiative

PURPOSE OF THIS TOOL

This final tool is a synthesis of the major themes and recommendations presented in this overall ASCD action tool. It can be used in multiple ways, but it can make an efficient handout for distribution to stakeholder groups to emphasize key Whole Child focus areas and recommended strategic planning processes to sustain momentum.

HOW TO USE THIS TOOL

You may wish to begin by using this tool as a discussion resource for an initial staff meeting or community meeting about the Whole Child Initiative. Another use is as a self-reflection tool in which staff members, community members, and students can discuss its key points and implications for improving the quality and performance of your school or district. It can also be used as a catalyst for reviewing and reflecting upon the levels of progress you have made throughout the year—or over multiple years—in working with the Whole Child process.

TIPS AND VARIATIONS

- ✓ Ask members of a department or grade level to reflect on their individual and collective progress on addressing the Whole Child process.
- ✓ Invite community members to respond to the ideas presented here and provide feedback about areas of perceived progress and areas of need.
- ✓ Use this tool as a catalyst for identifying community outreach and engagement activities (in conjunction with tools presented in each tenet-related section).

Checklist for Sustaining Momentum for Your Whole Child Initiative

Ensure that you view your Whole Child process as holistic and integrated, with each of the five tenets complementing one another and your overall vision. For example, how much consensus is present in your school or district about ways in which you are addressing the following?

- Your vision for your Whole Child work
- The meaning of the five Whole Child tenets for your school or district
- The big ideas within each of the tenets
- Your long-range goals and performance indicators for your Whole Child strategic plan
- The need for value-added evaluation
- The need for job-embedded professional development that emphasizes stakeholder involvement and inquiry via study groups, inquiry teams, and action research activities
- The importance of community outreach, engagement, and involvement

Be committed to the concept of distributed leadership, that is, empowering key individual stakeholders and stakeholder groups to assume leadership roles in the transformation process.

Strive to ensure that your written strategic plan is viable and realistic, with budgeted resources for materials, supplies, and technology, and staff time to assume the important but challenging components of your planning process.

Use the Concerns-Based Adoption Model (C-BAM) to support stakeholders as they move through the stages of concern when working with organizational changes:

- **Level 0 (Nonuse):** Initially, stakeholders may not know about or may take no action on any of the components of your Whole Child Initiative.
- **Level I (Orientation):** Eventually, stakeholders will begin to seek and acquire information about key aspects of the Whole Child Initiative.
- **Level II (Preparation):** The next phase involves stakeholders deciding to commit themselves to addressing the principles and strategies identified in the Whole Child Compact, as well as actively preparing to implement some or all of them.
- **Level III (Mechanical Use):** After stakeholders have made initial attempts to implement the core or basic strategies and processes associated with your Whole Child plan, they will sometimes feel that they need additional coaching, guidance, and reassurance about the quality of their use and their level of understanding.
- **Level IVa (Routine):** Next, stakeholders typically establish a satisfactory pattern for using the key strategies and processes associated with the Whole Child Initiative, but they need to extend and refine their understanding and use of them.
- **Level IVb (Refinement):** Stakeholders move on to considering themselves to be going beyond routine or mechanical use of the strategies and processes associated with key aspects of the Whole Child Initiative. They begin to assess

the impact of their use of the strategies and processes upon student achievement so that they can make appropriate modifications and improvements.
- **Level V (Integration):** Stakeholders then begin to actively collaborate and coordinate with others to use the strategies and processes of key aspects of your Whole Child Initiative both within and across grade levels and content areas.
- **Level VI (Renewal):** Finally, stakeholders should begin collaborating with other colleagues to find more effective alternatives for areas that may require enhancement or improvement in the collective use of the strategies and processes for the Whole Child Initiative and preparing every student for success.

References and Other Resources

American Youth Policy Forum & Association for Supervision and Curriculum Development. (2005). *Restoring the balance between academics and civic engagement in public schools.* Washington, DC: Authors.

Association for Supervision and Curriculum Development. (2007). The Learning Compact Redefined: A Call to Action. A Report of the Commission on the Whole Child. Alexandria, VA.

Barton, P. E. (2003, October). *Parsing the achievement gap.* Princeton, NJ: Educational Testing Service.

Blank, M., & Berg, A. (2006). *All together now: Sharing responsibility for the whole child.* A report for the Commission on the Whole Child convened by the Association for Supervision and Curriculum Development, Alexandria, VA. Available: http://www.ascd.org/ASCD/pdf/sharingresponsibility.pdf

Blum, R. (2005). *School connectedness: Improving students' lives.* Baltimore: Johns Hopkins Bloomberg School of Public Health.

Bridgeland, J. M., DiIulio, J. J., & Wulsin, S. C. (2008). *Engaged for success: Service-learning as a tool for high school dropout prevention.* Washington, DC: Civic Enterprises.

California Department of Education. (2005). *Getting results: Update 5—Student health, supportive schools, and academic success.* Sacramento, CA: CDE Press.

Center on Education Policy. (2006, March). *From the capital to the classroom: Year 4 of the No Child Left Behind Act.* Retrieved November 6, 2006, from http://www.cep-dc.org/nclb/Year4/CEP-NCLB-Report-4.pdf

Conference Board, Corporate Voices for Working Families, Partnership for 21st Century Skills, and Society for Human Resource Management. (2006). *Are they really ready to work? Employers' perspectives on the basic knowledge and applied skills of new entrants to the 21st century U.S. workforce.* Retrieved November 1, 2006, from http://www.conference-board.org/pdf_free/BED-06-Workforce.pdf

Fletcher, A. (2003). *Meaningful student involvement: Guide to inclusive school change.* Olympia, WA: The Freechild Project.

Fletcher, A. (2005). *Meaningful student involvement: Guide to students as partners in school change.* Olympia, WA: The Freechild Project; and Kenmore, WA: HumanLinks Foundation.

Gray, J., & Thomas, H. (2005). *If she only knew me.* Owensboro, KY: Rocket Publishing.

Hodgkinson, H. (2006). *The whole child in a fractured world.* For the Commission on the Whole Child convened by the Association for Supervision and Curriculum Development, Alexandria, VA. Available: http://www.ascd.org/ASCD/pdf/fracturedworld.pdf

Institute of Medicine. (2004). *Engaging schools: Fostering high school students' motivation to learn.* Washington, DC: National Academies Press.

Laitsch, D., Lewallen, T., & McCloskey, M. (2005, February). The whole child: Framework for education in the 21st century. *Infobrief, 40,* 1–8.

Learning First Alliance. (2001). *Every child learning: Safe and supportive schools.* Alexandria, VA: Association for Supervision and Curriculum Development.

Lichtenberg, J., Woock, C., & Wright, M. (2008). *Ready to innovate: Are educators and executives aligned on the creative readiness of the U.S. workforce?* New York: The Conference Board.

National Association of Secondary School Principals. (2004). *Breaking ranks II.* Reston, VA: Author.

National Governors Association. (2003). *Ready for tomorrow: Helping all students achieve secondary and postsecondary success—A guide for governors.* Washington, DC: Author.

National Middle School Association. (2006). *Success in the middle: A policymaker's guide to achieving quality middle level education.* Westerville, OH: Author.

Pearson, S. S. (2002). *Finding common ground: Service learning and education reform—A survey of 28 leading school reform models.* Washington, DC: American Youth Policy Forum.

Perkins, Brian. (2007). *Where we teach: The CUBE survey of urban school climate.* Alexandria, VA: National School Boards Association.

Pittman, K., Martin, S., & Williams, A. (2007). *Core principles for engaging young people in community change.* Washington, DC: The Forum for Youth Investment.

Rothstein, R. (2004). *Class and schools: Using social, economic, and educational reform to close the black-white achievement gap.* Washington, DC: Economic Policy Institute.

Schaps, E. (2006). *Educating the whole child.* For the Commission on the Whole Child convened by the Association for Supervision and Curriculum Development, Alexandria, VA.

Struck, C. (2006). *First Amendment Schools Project schools year-end report and accompanying documentation: Price Laboratory School.* Cedar Falls, IA: University of Northern Iowa.

Stewart, Vivien (2007, April) Becoming Citizens of the World. *Educational Leadership 64*(7), 9–14.

U. S. Department of Education, National Center for Education Statistics. (2005). *The condition of education 2005.* (NCES 2005–094). Washington, DC: U.S. Government Printing Office.

Wingspread declaration on school connections. (2004, September). *Journal of School Health, 74*(7), 233.